F O C U S

It's Not About the Fight But The Call

Betty Booker

FOCUS: It's Not About the Fight, But the Call is a powerful, Spirit-led guide for anyone walking through hardship, transition, or spiritual warfare. In this bold and honest book, Minister Betty Booker calls readers to shift their focus from life's battles to God's greater purpose.

Drawing on biblical truth, personal testimony, and heartfelt encouragement, Betty reminds us that while the struggle is real, the call is greater. Each chapter challenges you to examine what you're truly fighting, recognize distractions and deception, and remember that God often prepares us privately before positioning us publicly.

Whether you're wrestling with identity, betrayal, fear, or loss, this book invites you to realign your heart, renew your strength, and walk boldly in the assignment God has placed on your life. It's more than a book—it's a wake-up call for all to rise up, get focused, and finish their race with power, passion, and purpose.

This journey is deeply personal. Betty writes not from a place of perfection but from the trenches, where she has faced insecurity, grief, and rejection. Her transparency encourages you to bring your whole heart before God and stop performing for people because the call of God cannot be fulfilled with a divided heart.

FOCUS reminds us that while the fight has a purpose, it's not the destination. God doesn't just call the qualified—He qualifies the called. If you've ever questioned your purpose or your assignment, felt like giving up, or wondered if your fight disqualified you, this book is for you. You went through to become you.

It's time to refocus. It's time to rise. It's not about the fight—it's about the call.

Beyond The Book Media, LLC
Alpharetta. GA
www.beyondthebookmedia.com

The publisher is not responsible for websites
that are not owned by the publisher.

ISBN: 978-1-966430-21-6 (Print)

TABLE OF CONTENTS

DEDICATION

To everyone who has ever endured hard times, who may be in hard times, and for all who will face hard times, my sincere hope is that when reading or listening to this book, you will come to a place of knowing that in your life, you are more than where you are now. You are more than what has, is, and will happen to you and in your lives. All that happens and has happened is only to grow and direct you to a greater future and plan.

I pray that the words penned here and my life will inspire you to stretch and unceasingly fight for the someone greater in you, greater than me, and greater than any occurrence in your life.

Each time you face the most minor or significant challenge, keep your focus and believe in Christ Jesus!

FOREWORD

Being married to Betty for 26 years (2017), I have witnessed this book come to fruition through my life experiences, thoughts, and prayers.

This book is a survival manual that answers the questions: How can we quench our thirst while still thriving in a desert? How can we fight without knowing what we are fighting for? It's not about the fight but the call.

The attitude of winning or surviving the fight can consume us so much that we often know nothing about what we are fighting, who we are fighting, and why. Our call, purpose, and destiny are more important than the fight itself. THE CALL is to walk in the will for your life, be what you were born to be, and do it freely.

"You did not choose me, but I chose you and appointed you so that you might go and bear fruit-fruit that will last"(John 15:16, NIV).

As you read this book, I pray that you will be encouraged and strengthened to move past the fights and issues of life and move toward your call, purpose, and destiny.

"Therefore, since we are surrounded by such a great cloud of witnesses, let us throw off everything that hinders and the sin that so easily entangles. Don't be constrained with the process or in the process because beyond the barriers, there is life!!" (Hebrews 12:1, NIV).

Minister Victor Booker

INTRODUCTION

Since I can remember, my life has been a "fight." There has been one hard, super hard, unbearable, unbelievable thing, one disappointment, one heartbreak, and one lie after another. Do you know what I mean? I know I am not alone in feeling this way. We all have had disappointments and pain. I felt like no sooner than I finished fighting against one thing, another would pop up, and then another and another until I was living a life of fighting. Can I tell you how exhausting and draining that can be? I couldn't put one foot in front of the other in the middle of one fight. I didn't know if I was going to make it or collapse.

One Sunday, when I entered the church, someone asked me if they could speak with me; being in ministry, this happens quite often. So, I thought, sure, this was another opportunity to pray with someone, encourage someone, or give words of wisdom. I made my way into the room, and before I could close the door fully, she assaulted me with words: "I just wanted to tell you that I don't speak to you much because you think you are all that!!!" Her words meant she accused me of thinking I was better than others. She continued the confrontation, saying, "You think you are cute." I'm thinking, these are things people deal with when they are in the fifth grade. I was so confused.

I listened to her go on and on about me--what I think and how I act. And when she finished (I know, you are as shocked as I am that I let her finish), when she said her peace, my only response to the young lady was in the Spirit because, in the flesh, I would have had to say a whole lot more, me being me, I saw a few flashes of my hands around her neck. Will you say it with me? "But God!"

Here we were: two adults, two acquaintances, two church members, two leaders with no standing, and she was trying to tell me what I thought. I was somewhat surprised! While in reality, she seemed confrontational and dissatisfied, the truth was that she was seeing that I was different. The hand of God in my life had sparked some jealousy in her. The truth was that I was doing well.

The Spirit of the Lord took over, and all I could say to her at that moment, very calmly (that's how I know it was in the Spirit of God), was, "I really don't care what you think. I am on the wall. I am working for God. I am focused on the things of God. I am about my Father's business, and I am not coming down from this wall for you or for anyone else." (Nehemiah essentially said this when he was on assignment from the Lord.)

It is incredible how people will try to cause you to come down and step outside of God to stop doing God's work. They will tempt you to pull out of character, slip, and say something they can later use against you. The enemy will use people to upset you to the point that you revert to your old ways, act like a fool, and stop doing God's will.

When you try to be about the Father's business, people will say all manner of evil, and Satan will use anything he can to get your attention off of what you need to be thinking about. He'll even use kindergarten things like this, "You think you all that?! You think that you're better than everybody else?!" He has all kinds of gimmicks, tricks, and confusion to pull you away from what God has for your life.

You must focus on God, stay in the Spirit, and watch for Satan's tricks. Stay confident in yourself and what God has called you to do. People will try to make you feel wrong about being confident. Confidence is not arrogance; it is an assurance, a certainty that God is with you. You must be confident in what you believe God has called you to.

People will discourage you, talk about you, and put you down. They aim to hinder you and try everything in the book to trip you up, to stop you from being all that God called you to be.

In this fight of life, you must have a made-up mind. I will do what God has called me to do, and I'll do it even if you think I'm trying to outdo you. I'll do it even if you think I'm trying to be better than you. I'll do it even if you think I am trying to be cute. I will work as unto the Lord.

'Whatever you do, work at it with all your heart, as working for the Lord, not for human masters, since you know that you will receive an inheritance from the Lord as a reward. It is the Lord Christ you are serving."(Colossians 3:23-24, NIV)

CHAPTER 1

THERE WILL BE TRIBULATION

"I have told you these things, so that in me you may have peace. In this world you will have trouble. But take heart! I have overcome the world." (John 16:33, NIV)

Shocker! Who really wants to hear that life will come with distress, pressure, and hardship? Most of us would much rather be told that everything will work out, that life will be filled with comfort, success, and peace. But in John 16:33 (NIV), Jesus says plainly: You will have tribulation. He doesn't sugarcoat it. He doesn't say, You might. He says, You will.

Somewhere along the journey, we begin to believe that life is supposed to be easy, filled with smiles, sunny days, and smooth roads. As children, the world feels magical. Cartoons, cereal, laughter, snacks, and playtime fill our days. We live as if good things just appear—without thought, without effort, without cost. We enjoy blessings without ever realizing someone is behind them.

Then, life hits.

We face our first betrayal. Our first bully. Our first heartbreak or failure. We encounter loss, grief, and disappointment. And all at once, life no longer feels easy. We ask: Why is this so hard? Is it just me? Is something wrong with my faith? Jesus already gave us the answer:
"In this world, you will have trouble." This is the reality of every believer. As long as you're breathing, there will be seasons of tribulation. You might be misunderstood, mistreated, abandoned, or overlooked. You may suffer loss, illness, rejection, or grief so heavy it silences your words.

And here's the hard truth: Following Jesus doesn't eliminate the tribulation—sometimes, it intensifies it. Saying yes to God doesn't mean the storm won't come. In fact, sometimes storms arrive because you said yes. But even in the storm, there's purpose. Even in pain, there's divine intention. This may not sound like good news, but it is. Why? Because tribulation isn't meant to destroy you—it's meant to refine you. It shapes you. Grows you. Anchors you. It reveals the strength of God's presence in your life and makes you more like Him.

The truth is, most growth doesn't happen on the mountaintop. It happens in the valley. In the tension. In the questions. On the nights when you feel like giving up, but choose to trust anyway. The pain may not make sense, but it's not wasted. Even when you don't understand the "why," faith whispers: God is still working.

Take Jonah. He was called by God, but his disobedience landed him in a storm and eventually in the belly of a great fish. The storm wasn't sent to destroy him—it was sent to redirect him. To bring him back into alignment. Sometimes, God uses storms to shake us up, not to break us down. Not all storms are punishment—some are invitations. God loves you enough to disrupt your comfort in order to realign your purpose.

Jesus told us plainly: Tribulation is part of the journey. But He also gave us this promise: "Be of good cheer—I have overcome the world."

And because He overcame, you can too.

When the Message is Bigger than the Messenger

God wanted to save the people of Nineveh, but He also wanted to change Jonah's heart. Sometimes, God's purposes extend far beyond what we can see or understand. His plans often have greater depths than we can comprehend.

Even though Jonah initially resisted God's will, God did not give up on him. Through suffering and trials—enduring the storm, being thrown overboard, swallowed by a great fish, and finally being spat out onto dry land—Jonah was redirected back to obedience. God's grace was at work, shaping Jonah into a willing messenger.

This story reminds us that God's message is far bigger than any one person. Even when we are reluctant or flawed, God can use us to fulfill His plans. Sometimes, we might feel unworthy or unwilling, but God's call does not depend on our perfection—it depends on His power.

Jonah's journey teaches us that obedience is essential, even when we don't fully understand the mission or agree with the people involved. God's work often stretches us beyond our comfort zones, calling us to a purpose greater than ourselves.

Are you resisting God's call because it feels too hard, too scary, or because you doubt your own ability? Remember, God equips those He calls and can use you despite your doubts and fears. The message God wants to share through you is bigger than you, and that's a good thing.

CHAPTER 2

STORMY DECISIONS

Jonah was called to speak the word of the Lord—not just any word, but a pretty harsh one. God sent Jonah to a Gentile nation full of unsaved, evil people. Even so, God had a perfect plan for these Gentiles, revealing His love for all people, even those who seem farthest from Him. God's heart desires that everyone live a full life reconciled to Him.

Jonah received his assignment from the Lord: go to Nineveh, the capital city of the Assyrian empire, and proclaim God's warning against their wickedness. Understandably, this was difficult for Jonah—it would be difficult for anyone. Yet, instead of obeying, "But Jonah ran away from the Lord and headed for Tarshish. He went down to Joppa, where he found a ship bound for that port. After paying the fare, he went aboard and sailed for Tarshish to flee from the Lord"(Jonah 1:3, KJV).

Jonah ran away from what scared him.

He went down to Joppa and found a ship bound for Tarshish. His journey outside God was a downward spiral. Life is already hard, but when we choose disobedience over God's plan, we descend into even more trouble and pain. Jonah started "up," but his refusal to obey caused him to go down.

Running from God's call—hiding and refusing obedience—is something many of us relate to. We run in the opposite direction of God's will, only to face hardships we could have avoided. Jonah thought he could escape God's presence, but Psalm 139 reminds us: "Where can I go from your Spirit? Where can I flee from your presence?" (Psalm 139:7, NIV). There is no escape.

Jonah's heart was hardened. Maybe insecurities, fear, or apathy caused him to rebel. The call from God rarely looks like what we expect. It often leads us into uncomfortable valleys or turbulent seas. But disobedience also brings storms—storms we create ourselves.

As a result of running away, Jonah faced a violent storm that endangered everyone on the ship. His shipmates prayed to their gods, but none answered. Finally, they woke Jonah and asked, "Tell us, we pray thee, for whose cause this evil is upon us?" (Jonah 1:8, KJV). Jonah admitted he was the cause and told them to throw him overboard. Reluctantly, they did—and the storm calmed immediately.

Then came the fish.

Now the Lord provided a huge fish to swallow Jonah, and Jonah was in the belly of the fish three days and three nights" (Jonah 1:17, NIV). Imagine being swallowed by a fish—three days in darkness, with no escape. The stench, the pressure, and the suffocating darkness must have been terrifying. Jonah was trapped in a hard place—a place of darkness and despair. Have you ever felt that way? Caught in a situation so overwhelming you can barely breathe?

Inside the fish, Jonah cried out to God. And God heard him. The fish spit Jonah out onto dry land. Given a second chance, Jonah obeyed. He went to Nineveh and delivered God's message, despite his bitterness that the people deserved judgment, not mercy.

May we learn to obey quickly when God calls us out of our dark places. We don't always have to understand or agree with the call— we just need to obey for our good and the sake of those watching us. How are you like Jonah? Maybe you feel restless, sensing God has more for your life, but unsure what. Maybe fear, lack of resources, or uncertainty makes you hesitate or run away. But disobedience leads to storms.

Your disobedience not only affects your life, but it can also disturb the lives of those around you. Jonah's storm was dangerous to the whole ship.

Are you peacefully sleeping in disobedience, unaware of the damage it causes? Even if you rest well, that doesn't mean you're in God's will. Jonah slept while the ship was in chaos.

In the storm, pray and seek God's guidance. Trust his plan even when you can't see the outcome. God's ways are higher than ours.

God wanted to save the people of Nineveh, but He also wanted to change Jonah's heart. God's plans often stretch beyond what we can comprehend. Even when we resist, God's grace can shape us through trials.

Jonah's story shows that God's message is bigger than any one person. He can use us despite our flaws and fears. Obedience matters, even when we don't understand or like the mission.

Are you resisting God's call because it's scary or because you doubt yourself? Remember, God equips those He calls. The message you carry is bigger than you, and that's a good thing.

CHAPTER 3

WHAT ARE YOU FIGHTING?

A fight is anything that causes you to feel fear, discouragement, anger, distraction, or despair. Fights can take the form of abuse, addiction, rejection, or spiritual attacks. These things are designed to steal your focus from Jesus Christ and His promises of peace and joy. But those very same fights can also lead you to draw closer to God.

I've experienced intense battles in my life—the kind of battles that make you question everything you've believed. The weight of it all had me ready to give up on people, my calling, and even God. But even when I didn't have answers, even when my prayers felt unanswered, I refused to quit.

"For my thoughts are not your thoughts, neither are your ways my ways," declares the Lord..." — Isaiah 55:8 NIV

God's ways are not our ways. What we want isn't always what He wills. And what we imagine for ourselves often doesn't compare to the plans He's unfolding. Like Jonah, we must lay aside our own understanding and walk by faith.

The Enemy's Strategy

The enemy's goal is to wear you down. He won't turn you away from God all at once—he does it subtly, using doubt, fear, fatigue, and discouragement. He makes everything about you: Why me? Why now? Why this way? You become hyper-focused on your life and the outcomes you expect, and if those don't come to pass, despair creeps in.

The enemy digs into old wounds, stirring up shame, regret, and unforgiveness. He whispers lies that make you question your worth and your purpose. He plants confusion right at the crossroads of decision-making. But giving up is not an option. Changing direction isn't quitting. Adjusting the course is not failure. Sometimes, God redirects you because He has something greater in store.

Purpose in the Pain

Every obstacle, every hardship, and every heartbreak is meant to grow you spiritually and mentally. It's not easy to see suffering as an opportunity to grow, but with practice, we begin to understand that even in difficulty, God is with us. Challenges should draw us out of our comfort zone, strip away false expectations, and reveal God's direction.

I've faced seasons where everything hit at once—bills piling up, appliances breaking down, workplace struggles, strained relationships. It was disheartening. But in each season, I began to ask: What is this moment teaching me? What do I need to release?

What truth do I need to receive?

Adversity tries to either distract or deceive us. Distraction: Turning our attention away from God.

Deception: Making us believe what isn't true about God or ourselves.

These trials aren't meant to destroy us—they are meant to shape us and keep us aligned with God's voice and purpose.

A Fight for Confidence

I once held an academic admin position that I knew was from the Lord. I didn't have the credentials or the background, but God placed me there. At my first big meeting, I was terrified. Surrounded by people with advanced degrees, I felt out of place and inadequate. But as I dressed that morning, the Lord whispered, "You are adequate. You put your pants on the same way they do." That word reminded me—I am not less than. God placed me in that room for a reason, and He will give me everything I need.

Was I still nervous? Absolutely. But I went into that room knowing I belonged, not because of me, but because God assigned me. I worked in that position for over ten years, growing in confidence, knowledge, and faith. On my first day, God told me I'd be there for ten years. At the time, I brushed it off, but He was right. It was hard to leave because I loved what I did, but he was calling me to something else. .

Loss, Calling, and Obedience

In the middle of my career success, I was also experiencing deep personal loss. People I loved and trusted—friends and family—walked away. Some couldn't accept my calling. Others misunderstood me or judged me harshly. Even those I poured into with love and ministry left when I had nothing left to give.

I didn't know why the fight was so intense. But through it all, my husband Victor remained my covering and support. He prayed with me, encouraged me, and reminded me of what God was doing in my life.

Eventually, I left that job and stepped fully into ministry with all my heart. It was terrifying. The calling felt bigger than me, and anything I could do, I didn't know if I could endure the criticism, the pressure, or the sacrifices. But God reminded me that the message and the assignment He gave me was never about me—it was about Him.

I've been called "strong" and "tough," and maybe I am in some ways, but there are times in my own life when I don't feel that way. But more than that, I've learned to endure. I've learned to let negative words roll off and to press on through pain and confusion. I've learned to keep my eyes on the God who is greater than my circumstances.

There were times I didn't think I'd get back up—but I did, not because of my own strength but because of God's grace and purpose pushing me forward.

The night before I was to speak at a women's conference, I felt completely empty. I wasn't sure if I had heard from God. I was exhausted, overwhelmed, and paralyzed with fear. I even questioned everything-my preparation, my calling, my worthiness. As I sat in worship, surrounded by women, some of whom I deeply admired, I felt small, again, inadequate, and unworthy. I wanted to disappear, to call it off, to crawl into a corner and let someone more "qualified" take my place.

But when it was my time to stand. I stood to speak, trembling and unsure, I heard the Lord whisper to my spirit: "I called you, I called 80-year-old Moses, who had a stutter."

And for some reason, at that moment, I remembered: It's not about me. It never was.

God never needed me to be perfect. He didn't ask me to have it all together. He called me to be obedient. The fight at that moment wasn't against people—it was against fear, insecurity, and the lie that I wasn't enough. And while I was busy focusing on the fight within me, God was pointing me back to the call.

The call was to show up. The call was to speak what He gave me.

The call was to trust that His power is made perfect in my weakness.

The fight may be loud. The fear may be real. But the call is greater. And when we answer the call—despite the noise, despite the fear—God shows up through us. Because it was never about how worthy or ready I felt. It was always about His purpose, His message, and our yes.

So when you feel the pressure, when the battle is raging in your mind and your emotions, remember this:

The message is bigger than the messenger. The call is bigger than the conflict. God just needs your obedience.

When I felt empty, inadequate, and overwhelmed, that moment became a picture of what it means to FOCUS on the call, not the fight.

Focus means relying on His power, not your own capacity.

CHAPTER 4

FIRE CALLED

Seriously? It was fire that called Moses. If you were to take a moment and look at your life, look back over your life. What called you to be the person you are? What brought the best from you, what strengthened and humbled you? What trouble did you face even as a child? It was probably those things that began to prepare you. Look closer; it was fire, a fight, pain, or loss that built endurance and taught you to seek God and pray. Fire has a divine way of calling us.

God gave Moses everything he needed; his assignment was never about the fight—it was always about the call. When we examine Moses's life, we see a pattern of danger, deliverance, and divine design that began from infancy. God's plan for Moses was detailed and purposeful from the start.

When Pharaoh ordered all Hebrew baby boys to be killed, Moses' mother defied that command. She didn't just resist it—she risked everything to protect her son. Imagine the fear and determination it took to keep a baby silent for three months, knowing Egyptian soldiers or even frightened neighbors might report her. Yet, God gave her grace in those hidden months. And when hiding Moses was no longer possible, she took a bold step of faith—she let him go.

Saving Moses meant surrendering him. Letting go of her child couldn't have been easy. The dangers were countless: he could've drowned, been eaten by a predator, or been captured and killed. But with faith, she placed him in a basket she had carefully prepared to blend with the riverbank. That was no ordinary basket—it was an act of prophetic obedience. She let the current carry him, trusting that God's hand was greater than hers.

God, indeed, had a plan.

Because of that one courageous act, Moses was delivered into the hands of Pharaoh's daughter—an unlikely place of refuge. He was raised in the palace of the very man who ordered his death.

From the riverbank to royalty, Moses was protected because he was called. And because his mother trusted God beyond what she could see or understand, God honored her obedience.

This wasn't just about Moses surviving—it was about him being positioned for purpose.

Moses' calling was preserved even as an infant because God knew the end from the beginning. Though Jochebed surely wept and feared for her son, her obedience led Moses into the very hands that would raise him, educate him, and ultimately launch him into his divine assignment: to confront Pharaoh and deliver Israel.

Now, this is where we might think the fight begins. But again, it's not about the fight—it's about the call.

Even though Moses was older, slow of speech, and uncertain, he obeyed God. Time after time, he went to Pharaoh and said exactly what God told him to say: "Let my people go" (Exodus 7, NIV). Pharaoh repeatedly said no. The people suffered more. The labor grew harder. And Moses likely questioned everything.

What do you do when you obey God, but things get worse?

Moses' obedience seemed to bring more suffering for the Israelites. Pharaoh retaliated, increasing their workload and making their lives unbearable. Can you imagine the Israelites, already tired and oppressed, now working longer hours with fewer resources because Moses spoke up?

They didn't understand what was happening. They couldn't hear God. They didn't see Moses as a messenger. All they felt was pain. They were discouraged, broken, and had lost hope. And so many of us have been there—doing all we know to do, staying faithful, yet watching life get harder.

Sometimes, obedience leads to opposition before it leads to victory.

Each time Moses went to Pharaoh, he was rejected. But Pharaoh wasn't rejecting Moses—he was rejecting God. Moses, however, began to focus on the fight. He saw the hardship, the resistance, the repeated "no's."

He cried out to God:
"Why, Lord, why have you brought trouble on this people? Is this why you sent me? Ever since I went to Pharaoh to speak in your name, he has brought trouble on this people, and you have not rescued your people at all"(Exodus 5:22-23, NIV).

Obeying God and being in purpose can be extremely hard. God responded not with sympathy, but with power.

"Now you will see what I will do to Pharaoh: Because of my mighty hand he will let them go; because of my mighty hand he will drive them out of his country. God also said to Moses, "I am the Lord"(Exodus 6:1-2, NIV)

Now you will see. It is hard so you can see God. If it's too easy or too comfortable, you'll think you did something. You may think you are the one with the power.

It was never about Pharaoh. It was never about the plagues or the bricks or the "no's." It was always about the power of God working through a willing vessel. Moses was just the messenger—God was the mover.

God would eventually tell Moses:
"See, I have made thee a god to Pharaoh" (Exodus 7:1, NIV).
And yes, Pharaoh did finally let the people go—but only after devastating loss, including the death of his firstborn. The Israelites left in haste, victorious at last. But soon, Pharaoh changed his mind again and chased after them with his army. Once again,

fear rose. Once again, it seemed like God had abandoned them. But He hadn't.

Even when the enemy is chasing you down, God has already prepared your escape.

God led the Israelites, not along the shortest route, but the safest one—because He knew their hearts. If they faced war too soon, they might turn back. And isn't that just like us? We want easy, but God wants endurance. We want quick, but God wants character.

Those hard, confusing paths? They're often the ones that grow us the most. When you're facing final exams, struggling through a required class that's hard to understand, and dealing with a professor who seems like they're from another planet, remember, even this has a purpose in your journey.

All of these are tough paths. Believe it, these paths are making you strong and giving you endurance and tenacity.

And when the Israelites reached the Red Sea with Pharaoh's army closing in, God said something so striking:
"Why are you crying out to me? Tell the Israelites to move on" (Exodus 14:15, NIV).

At first, I thought God's words to Moses were harsh.
"Why are you crying out to me?" (Exodus 14:15, NIV).

I mean—who else are we supposed to cry out to in times of trouble?

But as I sat with that verse, I started to understand. There are moments when crying out isn't the problem, but staying stuck there is. There are times when we've already prayed, already cried, already sought God—and now it's time to act. You can spend so much time pleading with God that you miss the moment to move in faith, using what He's already given you.

It reminded me of how I raised my children.

I used to tell them, "When I ask you to do something, I need you to move quickly." It wasn't meant to be mean. It wasn't to be harsh. It was to protect them, because what if we were ever in danger? What if the house were on fire? What if I needed them to run for help or escape while I dealt with the threat?

Even the small things mattered. Pick up your shoes. Close the door. Don't answer it when someone knocks; wait for us.

It may have seemed minor at the time, but those instructions were training. I needed them to not only hear our voice but also know our voice and respond without delay.

I don't even like horror movies, but I've seen enough suspense films to know how it goes—when danger hits, it's not the time to ask questions. It's not the time to freeze or panic. When someone yells, "Run!"—you run. When they say, "Jump!"—you jump.

You don't say, "But I'm scared," or "I don't think I can." You trust the voice that's leading you. You trust the one you're with. And you move.

It took me a while to understand what God was really saying to Moses. But now I hear it clearly.

"Why are you crying out to Me?" Why are you standing still? Why are you frozen in fear? Why are you paralyzed in the middle of the breakthrough? I've already given you what you need. I've put the power in your mouth. Speak. Act. Use what's in your hand. Tell the people to move.

This wasn't the time for Moses to panic—it was the time to believe. To walk forward. To act in faith. To lead even while trembling.

And the same is true for you.

Sometimes, faith doesn't wait for fear to leave. Sometimes, faith moves in the middle of fear. This is not the time to panic. This is the time to move.

God commands Moses to "Raise your staff and stretch out your hand over the sea to divide the water so that the Israelites can go through the sea on dry ground." (Exodus 14:16 NIV).

That same staff Moses held when he was called at the burning bush, he now lifted again to see God perform a miracle. Lift what God has already given you. Trust Him to move. And move He did.

The waters parted. The Israelites walked through walls of water on dry ground. What seemed impossible became a pathway. What seemed like defeat turned into deliverance. And the very enemy that chased them was drowned in the sea behind them.

The Israelites were filled with awe before God and put their faith in Him (Exodus 14:31 NIV, paraphrased).

Just like Moses, just like the Israelites, you may feel overwhelmed by the fight in front of you. You may question the delay, the opposition, the pain. But it's not about the fight. It's always about the call.

"Now faith is confidence in what we hope for and assurance about what we do not see" (Hebrews 11:1, NIV).

God was faithful to His promise to Israel, and He will be faithful to you. Even when it looks like He's forgotten you. Even when the way is hard. Even when fear grips you.

The call is bigger than the crisis. The purpose is greater than the pain.

So, when God says move, move. And when He says, be still—be still. Because He's the one who fights for you, and His power will always make a way

Moses' story reminds us that when God calls you, He also equips you. The journey won't always be easy. In fact, like Moses, you may face resistance from others, discouragement from within, and spiritual battles that seem overwhelming. But it's not about the fight—it's about the call.

Just like Moses, you may feel unqualified. You may face setbacks, delays, or repeated "no's." You may not understand why things get harder when you're doing exactly what God told you to do.

But God is not absent in your struggle. He is refining you through the fire, preparing you to walk in authority and power, and proving His faithfulness through your obedience. Your Red Sea moment will come. Your Pharaoh will fall. What looks like a delay is often God setting the stage for a miracle.

So, what do you do now?

Surrender the fear. Trust that God sees the full picture even when you don't. Stay obedient. Keep saying "yes" even when it's difficult. Use what's in your hand. God has already given you the tools for your purpose. Move forward in faith. Don't freeze in fear—stand still in trust and then move when He says move.

This chapter explores the life of Moses, emphasizing that his journey was never about the battles he faced but about the divine call on his life. From infancy, Moses' life was marked by God's protection and purpose. Even when he was placed in a basket on the Nile, God orchestrated every detail for his preservation and future assignment.

Despite Moses' fears, insecurities, and repeated rejection by Pharaoh, God remained faithful to His word. Moses' obedience—through fear, frustration, and failure—reveals that the power to fulfill our calling comes not from our strength but from God's authority and presence. The repeated no's from Pharaoh weren't rejections of Moses but rejections of God's command. Yet Moses continued, trusting that God's plan would prevail.

As the Israelites faced intensified labor, impossible circumstances, and even moments of doubt, God was working behind the scenes. When Pharaoh's army pursued them, and fear gripped their hearts, Moses reminded them to "just stay calm" and trust in the Lord. The parting of the Red Sea was not just a miracle—it was a confirmation that God fights for those who are called.

The story of Moses teaches us that it's not about the fight we face but about the call we carry. God uses our most painful places to display His power and fulfill His promises.

The Spirit of the Fight

Even though the title of this book is FOCUS: It's Not About the Fight but the Call, let me be clear: the fight is still important. You must fight to remain in God's will and complete His plan for your life.

Some may say there's already enough fighting in the world—and I completely agree. There is more than enough violence, hurt, division, and destruction around us. But the fight I'm talking about is not with one another. This is a spiritual fight—a war in the unseen realm. And sadly, not enough of that kind of fighting is happening.

If we want to stand firm in our calling, if we want to obey what God has commanded us to do, we must fight.

There is a real adversary who is not only fighting you but is also threatening your family, your past, and your future generations. There's a war for your soul, your mind, your peace, and your purpose. And if you do not engage in that fight, you cannot complete your earthly assignment.

This doesn't mean earthly struggles don't matter. The fight for justice, the courage to stand against evil, and the conviction to speak for the voiceless do matter. Scripture tells us plainly:
"Speak (Open your mouth) for those who cannot speak for themselves, for the rights of all who are destitute." (Proverbs 31:8-9, NIV).

You will face hard conversations and unwelcome opinions. Not every comment, lie, or false assumption deserves your energy, but some do. You must know when to speak, when to pray, and when to press on in focused obedience. Do not let distractions or discouragement keep you from walking in what God has assigned to your life.

This is why Paul said:
"Finally, be strong in the Lord and in his mighty power. Put on the full armor of God, so that you can take your stand against the devil's schemes." (Ephesians 6:10-11, NIV).

That word "finally" is powerful. "Finally," comes after you've tried to figure it out, fix it, and fight it your way. "Finally," is when you say, "Enough—I must be strong in the Lord." This is your final stance, your final faith. Your belief must say: I will be strong in the Lord.

Understanding the Fight

Fights aren't just arguments or confrontations. A fight can be anything that makes you fearful, aggravated, distracted, disappointed, oppressed, or hurt. It can be abuse, addiction, manipulation, rejection, intimidation, shame, or lies. Fights try to break your focus, but they can also push you closer to God.

In my life, the consistency of pain, confusion, and betrayal pushed me to seek relief. I wanted to give up. At times, I drifted far from what I knew about God. Yet in all of it, He never left me.

I've seen God heal my body from COVID and thyroid cancer. I've seen Him provide for my family in miraculous ways. And still, during the most difficult trials—when I was tempted to give up—God was still there. Even when I didn't have answers... I kept pressing. Even when prayer didn't seem to change things... I kept believing. Even when I felt forsaken... I refused to give in.

"For my thoughts are not your thoughts, neither are your ways my ways," declares the LORD."(Isaiah 55:8, NIV).

God's way is rarely the way we envision. We want easy. We want visible progress. But God wants obedience. Just like Jonah, we must forget what we want and follow God by faith, not sight.

The Enemy's Strategy

Satan won't always launch a full-out attack—he often moves in subtle ways. Doubt. Fear. Weariness. He wants you to look inward, to feel overwhelmed and self-focused. He whispers, "Why me? I should be further along. Nothing's working." Before long, you're consumed with discouragement and comparison.

But hear me: you are not stuck. God can shift your path, open a door, or send help right in the middle of your breakdown. Don't mistake divine redirection for failure. Sometimes, a "no" from God is an invitation to grow stronger and trust deeper.

The enemy thrives on two tactics:
Distraction: shifting your attention from God to circumstances. Deception: convincing you that what God said is not true. After accepting my call to preach, the warfare intensified. People walked away. Friends turned cold. Family became distant. I was misunderstood, misjudged, and misrepresented. Those I poured

into left. And just when I thought I had nothing left to give, the Lord reminded me: The call will cost you something. But you are not alone, and though I didn't understand it all at the time, He was preparing me for ministry.

When the Fight Feels Too Big

There were times I questioned everything. I didn't know if I had what it took. The lies, the accusations, the exhaustion—it was overwhelming. I didn't feel strong or smart. But my husband, Victor, covered me in prayer, spoke life over me, and reminded me of God's promises. He saw the God in me when I couldn't. Ministry didn't make things easier. If anything, the fight became more intense. I was leading others, pouring out while trying to hold myself together. But God sustained me through every rejection, betrayal, and loss. I kept going. Even when I didn't understand. Even when I couldn't hear Him clearly. Even when I felt like quitting. I. Kept. Going. I fought with focus.

Every obstacle is an opportunity to see God more clearly. When the money is low, the A/C breaks, the roof leaks, the boss mistreats you—those are the very moments where God can show His strength.

I've learned to ask God questions. Lord, what is this moment teaching me? I know there is something I can learn from this. Something that can help me now or later. But there is a lesson in it all. I've learned to ask, Lord, what do I need to release or let go of? I've also learned that sometimes, there are things I need to let go of. Maybe it's a relationship, a habit, a way of thinking. And, I have learned to ask the Lord, "How can I glorify you in this? Lord, I desire to give you glory."

In this situation, how can I do that? You are not without help. God has not left you. And when it seems the hardest, He is often the closest.

Identifying Fights – Things That Distract and Deceive

Even though the title of this book is Focus: It's Not About the Fight, But the Call, the fight still matters. You will have to fight—and stay focused—if you're going to remain in God's will and complete what He has assigned to your life.

You will have to fight for your rights. You will have to let people know that you will not be disrespected or mishandled. You will have to fight to keep going when those who should lift you up and support you instead join in tearing down your character and assignment. You will have to fight to separate yourself from the negative and the lazy so you can press forward.

You will have to fight for the cause, which is Christ and the assignment He has placed on your life. You matter. And if you're going to get to the place where you can truly say, "It's not about the fight, but the call," you must be sure of your calling. Sure, of your assignment. Sure, of the Word of God and His promises over your life. "Therefore, my brothers and sisters, make every effort to confirm your calling and election. For if you do these things, you will never stumble."(2 Peter 1:10, NIV).

There's already enough violence in this world. I agree with that. On the earth, there is enough killing, hurting, and destroying of one another. But this fight—the one I'm talking about—is not against people. It's a spiritual fight. And in the spirit realm, there is not enough fighting. If we're going to stand firm in our calling and obey what God has commissioned us to do, we must learn to fight in the Spirit.

There is a real adversary threatening you, your family, your generational future, and the legacy of those who came before you. This is a war for your soul, your peace, your clarity, and your purpose. If you refuse to fight, you will not complete your earthly assignment. Paul made this plain when he wrote to the church in Ephesus:
In John 10:10, it states, "The thief comes only to steal and kill and destroy. I came that they may have life and have it abundantly." Let

me be clear—I'm not saying that the fights we face on earth don't matter. There are times when you will need to take a stand, confront injustice, and defend what's right. Stand up for yourself.

Sometimes, people and circumstances will confront you, attacking your name, dismissing your voice, and excluding you because of who you are. And in those moments, yes, you may have to speak up and fight back.

Saying that our life is "not about the fight" does not mean we pretend there is no fight at all. Listen to me—we must fight. You'll hear me say it more than once in this book: You must fight. I am here because I refused to believe the lie that I wasn't enough. I am smart enough. I know enough. I am worthy of being heard. I am worthy of joy, peace, and love—and so are you.

Don't let giving up become your default. Don't let fear, intimidation, or shame silence you. I've watched too many people live in defeat—addicted, angry, depressed, isolated, bitter, tearing others down in order to feel lifted up themselves.

We must press forward. We must remain focused. We cannot allow anything to interrupt, intervene, hinder, or stop what God has for our lives. And sometimes, that means we have to fight.

"Finally, my brethren, be strong in the Lord and in the power of His might. Put on the whole armor of God, that ye may be able to stand against the wiles of the devil" — Ephesians 6:10-11 (NIV)

That word "finally" isn't just about the end. It's your turning point. It's the "but" before the next battle. It's the "now" before the next test. You have to say to yourself: Finally, I will be strong in the Lord and in the power of His might. When that settles in your spirit—when your final word is faith—you can face any fight that comes, whether spiritual, emotional, or physical.

Recognize your fights

Fights aren't always obvious. They're not just about conflict with people. A fight can be anything that causes you to feel fearful, angry, discouraged, or distracted. Fights may show up as:

ABUSE

"For our struggle is not against flesh and blood, but against the rulers, against the authorities, against the powers of this dark world and against the spiritual forces of evil in the heavenly realms."
— (Ephesians 6:12, NIV).

ADDICTIONS

"But I see another law at work in me, waging war against the law of my mind and making me a prisoner of the law of sin at work within me."
(Romans 7:23, NIV).

REJECTION

"Though my father and mother forsake me, the Lord will receive me."
(Psalm 27:10, NIV).

INTIMIDATION

"No weapon forged against you will prevail, and you will refute every tongue that accuses you. This is the heritage of the servants of the Lord, and this is their vindication from me," declares the Lord.
(Isaiah 54:17, NIV).

EMOTIONAL TRAUMA

"The weapons we fight with are not the weapons of the world. On the contrary, they have divine power to demolish strongholds. We demolish arguments and every pretension that sets itself up against the knowledge of God..."
(2 Corinthians 10:4-5, NIV).

LIES SPOKEN OVER YOUR LIFE

"You belong to your father, the devil, and you want to carry out your father's desires. He was a murderer from the beginning, not holding to the truth, for there is no truth in him. When he lies, he speaks his native language, for he is a liar and the father of lies."
(John 8:44, NIV).

HOMELESSNESS

"We are hard pressed on every side, but not crushed; perplexed, but not in despair; persecuted, but not abandoned; struck down, but not destroyed." (2 Corinthians 4:8-9, NIV).

GENERATIONAL PATTERNS OF DYSFUNCTION

"You shall not bow down to them or worship them; for I, the Lord your God, am a jealous God, punishing the children for the sin of the parents to the third and fourth generation of those who hate me, but showing love to a thousand generations of those who love me and keep my commandments." (Exodus 20:5-6, NIV).

FEAR

"For the Spirit God gave us does not make us timid, but gives us power, love and self-discipline."
(2 Timothy 1:7, NIV).

JOBLESSNESS

"But seek first his kingdom and his righteousness, and all these things will be given to you as well."
(Matthew 6:33, NIV).

SEASONS OF LONELINESS AND ISOLATION

"Be alert and of sober mind. Your enemy the devil prowls around like a roaring lion looking for someone to devour. Resist him, standing firm in the faith…"
(1 Peter 5:8-9, NIV).

FRUSTRATIONS

"For the flesh desires what is contrary to the Spirit, and the Spirit what is contrary to the flesh. They are in conflict with each other, so that you are not to do whatever you want."
(Galatians 5:17, NIV).

ANGER

"Because human anger does not produce the righteousness that God desires."
(James 1:20, NIV).

Fights are the things that try to pull your eyes away from Jesus Christ and distract you from God's Word, His promises, and His peace. Sometimes, the fight can be internal: your identity, your worth, your voice, your calling. And these are just as real as the external ones.

I know because I've lived them.

There was a season in my life where the fight felt constant—trouble, pain, lack, frustration—and it all seemed so heavy at the moment. I was doing everything I could just to survive, to overcome, to keep moving. I wanted to give up. I thought of doing something to help me get over it: get another job, lie on an application. I thought about walking away from everything -- my faith, my calling, my identity in Christ -- and just going back to the world.

Thank God, He kept me. Thank God it was just a thought. Thank God I didn't act on what I felt in the moment... I held on. I couldn't see it at the time, but God was still there. He was still providing. He was still healing. He was still opening doors and making ways. He still had a plan. I've seen God heal the sick—I am a testimony. I've seen God restore marriages, provide when there was no provision, and come through in moments that felt impossible.

Still, the pain made me want to quit. But the call pulled me closer to the Father. I stayed focused on His Word, and I stayed connected to mentors—people who loved the Lord and could speak wisdom, hope, and encouragement into my life. In those moments, it was their presence and their prayers that helped me stay focused and not get lost in my feelings.

Don't Confuse Feelings with Finality

Feeling like giving up and actually giving up are two very different things. Just because you feel weary doesn't mean it's over. Just because you're discouraged doesn't mean you've failed. You may have prayed fervently, fasted faithfully, and cried until you had no more tears, but still, it seems like nothing is changing. The silence is deafening. But hear me clearly: silence is not the same as absence. God is still working—even when you can't see it, feel it, or explain it.

We often confuse emotional exhaustion with spiritual defeat. But emotions are temporary—they are real, but they are not the authority. God's Word is. Your feelings may say, "It's over." God says, "I'm just getting started." Your heart may whisper, "You're alone." But the Spirit affirms, "I will never leave you nor forsake you."

"For My thoughts are not your thoughts, neither are your ways My ways," declares the Lord." (Isaiah 55:8, NIV).

God's way is rarely the path we would have chosen.

How many times have you wanted something so badly—prayed for it, hoped for it, even planned around it—only for God to close the door? At the time, it felt like a setback. But later, you saw why He said no. God had something better, something greater, something you couldn't have seen then.

Aren't you glad God didn't give you what you thought you needed? Looking back, you can see His protection in every "no," His wisdom in every delay, and His faithfulness in every detour. What felt like rejection was really redirection. What felt like loss was actually love in disguise.

His timing often stretches us, His process refines us, and His will requires us to lay down our expectations. Like Jonah, we sometimes wrestle with what we thought God would do—what we wanted Him to do. But spiritual maturity means surrendering what we expected in order to embrace what God has ordained.

Don't mistake delay for denial. Don't confuse hardship with abandonment. You are not forgotten. You are being molded and prepared. So, trust what God said—especially when your emotions say otherwise. Trust what He revealed to you in the secret place, even when your surroundings don't yet reflect it. Trust the vision He gave, the confirmation you received, the Scripture that leaped off the page into your heart. His plan is perfect. He is not a man that He should lie. He will reveal His purpose in His perfect time.

Hold on—not to the outcome you imagined, but to the One who holds the outcome in His hands.

Your feelings are real, but God's truth is final.

God's way is rarely the path we would have chosen.

How many times have you wanted something so badly—prayed for it, hoped for it, even planned around it—only for God to close the door? At the time, it felt like a setback. But later, you saw why He said no. God had something better, something greater, something you couldn't have seen then.

Aren't you glad God didn't give you what you thought you needed? Looking back, you can see His protection in every "no," His wisdom in every delay, and His faithfulness in every detour. What felt like rejection was really redirection. What felt like loss was actually love in disguise.

CHAPTER 5

DISTRACTION AND DECEPTION

The enemy's greatest weapon is distraction and deception. Every negative circumstance you face has one of two goals: to distract or to deceive you. Distraction pulls your attention away from God and His promises. It shifts your eyes toward things that are outside His will. It causes you to obsess over what's going wrong instead of focusing on what God is doing right.

Distraction makes noise louder than truth. Deception, on the other hand, attacks your belief system. It causes you to believe what is not true. Deception speaks lies to your soul and dresses them up as facts. It twists God's Word and tries to convince you that your identity, your future, and your worth are something less than what God has declared.

You must know who you are and whose you are. You are made in the image and likeness of the Father. He has made you unique and wonderful just as you are, and for any adjustments, He will guide you on what and when to make them. You must be your authentic self.

Authenticity says: "I don't need to be everywhere, do everything, or please everyone—I just need to be where God has placed me, doing what He's called me to do."

You don't need to chase false versions of success or compare your path to others, but focus on your calling and not be sidetracked by the noise or chaos around you. Distraction loses power because you know what matters, and your heart is anchored in purpose, not performance or people-pleasing.

I've learned that authenticity exposes deception. When you're authentic, you're aligned with God's truth about you, not the lies the enemy wants you to believe. Deception thrives in confusion and insecurity. But when you're grounded in who God says you are, you can spot a lie from a mile away, no matter who brings it, because your authentic identity is built on the word of the Lord, not circumstance, emotion, family, or public opinions.

Your Authenticity declares, "I am who God says I am—nothing more, nothing less. I don't have to prove, perform, or pretend." When you live authentically, you become a threat to the enemy because you're living focused, rooted, and free."

"No weapon formed against you shall prosper, and every tongue which rises against you in judgment you shall condemn" (Isaiah 54:17, NIV).

Being your Authentic Self

Being your authentic self is an act of spiritual resistance. Oh yes, because authenticity is warfare. Every time you choose truth over appearance, purpose over pressure, and identity over insecurity, you are resisting the enemy's tactics of distraction and deception. Distraction wants you busy performing. Authenticity keeps you grounded in purpose. When you're authentic, you're living from the inside out, not the outside in. You're not chasing what looks good to others—you're pursuing what God planted in you.

Authenticity says, "I choose who God made me to be, not who the world says I should be."

When you're walking in truth, your motivations are pure. You're not performing for approval—you're moving with conviction.

You can't run your race with power if you're constantly switching lanes, trying to impress the crowd. Remain in your lane.

You can't keep changing lanes forever, but you can sustain purpose when you're living from your true identity in Christ.

Purpose becomes exhausting when it's tied to performance—trying to please this one and fit in with that one, but when you're rooted in authenticity, it becomes life-giving.

God anoints the real you, not the version you think people want.

Deception wants you to doubt your worth. Authenticity stands firm in who God says you are, even when life says otherwise. Spiritual resistance doesn't always look like fighting demons. Sometimes, it looks like waking up and choosing to walk in your God-given identity, even when it's uncomfortable, unpopular, or unseen. You will not be liked or accepted when you are authentic about how God made you and what He called you to.

Authenticity is resistance. Identity is warfare. Focus is your victory.

D.O.N.T. Misjudge Your Fight

D – Don't give in to distractions and Doubt God's plan.

You misjudge your fight when you start believing God has forgotten you. The delay, the silence, or the hardship may tempt you to think you're off track—but God's plan often includes seasons that don't make sense to our natural mind.

Every fight has noise, but not every noise deserves your attention. Stay fixed on what God told you. Don't believe God has forgotten you. The delay, the silence, or the hardship may tempt you to think you're off track—but God's plan often includes seasons that don't make sense to our natural mind.

"Trust in the Lord with all your heart and lean not on your own understanding; in all your ways submit to him, and he will make your paths straight." (Proverbs 3:5-6, NIV).

O – Overcome with obedience and overestimate the opposition.

Victory isn't always loud. Sometimes, it's quietly doing what God said—even when it's hard. You misjudge the fight when you see your enemy as bigger than your God. Like the Israelites feared Goliath, it's easy to focus on the size of the problem instead of the strength of the One who's with you.

"If God is for us, who can be against us?" (Romans 8:31, NIV).

N – Never forget the call, and never neglect your spiritual weapons.

When emotions rise and pressure hits, remember what you're fighting for. God called you for this. You misjudge your fight when you try to fight in your own strength, forgetting that your real weapons are spiritual—prayer, the Word, faith, and worship. You're not in a flesh-and-blood battle; don't bring carnal tools to a spiritual war.

"For the weapons of our warfare are not of the flesh (carnal) but have divine power (through God) to destroy strongholds..." (2 Corinthians 10:4, NIV).

T – Turn your eyes to Jesus, and don't take it personal.

Refocus your heart on the One who fights for you. His presence is your peace, His word your weapon. You misjudge the fight when you make it about people or emotions. The enemy wants you to be offended, bitter, or distracted by the actions of others. But your fight is not with them—it's about what God has called you to do. "We wrestle not against flesh and blood..." (Ephesians 6:12, NIV). People may look at you and assume you're not qualified, just like Saul did to David before he faced Goliath. But they weren't there when you cried alone. They didn't see you pick yourself up after rejection. They don't know the nights you prayed through tears or the mornings you showed up when you had every reason to stay in bed.

They weren't there when God gave you the strength to stand up broken.

They didn't see you press forward with a limp and a word from God.

They didn't see you rise, not because you felt strong, but because you knew you were called.

You are in a fight, but not just any fight. You are in a focused, God-ordained, purpose-driven war for your calling. But you're not fighting alone. The Spirit of God is in you. His Word is your weapon. And your endurance is part of your testimony.

CHAPTER 6

PREPARED IN HARDSHIP

Being a champion doesn't come without pain or adversity. When David showed up at the Israelite camp to deliver lunch to his brothers, per his father Jesse's request, he had no idea he was walking into a divine confrontation. There he was—young, overlooked, and unarmed—standing before a giant named Goliath (1 Samuel 17, NIV). Goliath was called a champion because he had never lost a fight. He was a master of intimidation and warfare. But Goliath had never met David, a man of God who had already been prepared in obscurity.

David was a shepherd boy—alone in the fields, protecting sheep from wild beasts, guiding them to nourishment and safety, and fighting off predators. Through this daily work, David became tough yet compassionate. He learned to defend the vulnerable. His courage to stand against Goliath came not only from his compassion for his people but from his deep love for the Lord.

David had learned in the field that God was with him, and he believed that the same God would still be with him now.

What have you gone through that has prepared you for divine purpose?

Everything you need is within. Everything you need, you have learned through every experience, the good and the bad.

When no one saw your struggle, when no one knew your name, when people overlooked your potential, God was working. Every disappointment, every tear, every moment of silence was strategic. God was preparing your heart, shaping your mentality, strengthening your motivation, and refining your spirit to stand firm where He was calling you.

You weren't thrown into hardship; perhaps hardship was part of the call that prepared you.

David wasn't thrown into battle—he answered God's call after

God had equipped him. While tending his father's sheep, he encountered lions and bears. When they attacked, David struck them down and rescued what was his to protect. When the call came to fight Goliath, David volunteered. He wasn't fearless because he was reckless—he was fearless because he trusted the God who had never failed him before.

What you've already faced gives you the courage to show up. David was a young man, only about six feet tall, now standing before a battle-hardened warrior nearly nine feet tall. His brothers were present, as were others in the army, but none dared to face the giant. David was willing to fight, but he still had more to learn about himself. Alone in the field, he had learned what to do when faced with overwhelming odds. His assignment had been to protect the sheep—even at the risk of his life—and he remained faithful to that calling.

David likely learned how to strategize in the wilderness. Maybe he learned how to use the stones God provided. His vision was reshaped through his experiences: the lion and the bear made Goliath seem not so big after all. Every past victory should give us a new vision for the next challenge. If God brought you through that season, then you can stand again, with confidence, with clarity, and with the courage that God will bring you through once more.

David reassured King Saul, who doubted him, saying:
"Your servant has killed both the lion and the bear; this uncircumcised Philistine will be like one of them...The Lord who rescued me from the paw of the lion and the paw of the bear will rescue me from the hand of this Philistine" (1 Samuel 17:36-37, KJV).

Still, Saul insisted on dressing David in his own armor. David tried, but he couldn't walk in it—it wasn't made for him. The armor didn't fit, and it didn't belong to him.

Be your authentic self.

Trying to be someone you're not only hinders your ability to walk out God's call. If David had gone into battle dressed like Saul, the people would have credited the armor, not God. Saul could have claimed the victory as his own: "If it hadn't been for me..." But David knew better. He said, "This isn't me. God prepared me in the field, and I must fight like me." So, he removed Saul's armor and went into battle dressed like David.

David stopped by the stream, picked up five smooth stones, and armed himself with the slingshot he used daily as a shepherd. He stood before Goliath and declared, "You come against me. But I come against you in the name of the Lord Almighty, the God of the armies of Israel, whom you have defied. This very day... the whole world will know that there is a God in Israel...for the battle is the Lord's, and he will give all of you into our hands" (1 Samuel 17:45-47, NIV).

Whether David was declaring, decreeing, or simply building up his faith, he did what was necessary to win. Then he reached into his bag, pulled out a stone, swung his slingshot, and hit Goliath with deadly precision. The stone struck Goliath in the forehead and dropped the giant face-first to the ground. God gave David the victory, and one more step toward fulfilling his divine call.

David resisted the expectations and advice of experienced soldiers. He fought with what God gave him and with those who were with him. Some of us are fighting longer and harder because we're trying to fight like someone else. We're exhausted because we've been trying to wear someone else's armor.

Look back over your life—failed relationships, detours, disappointments, victories. God has used it all. Often, we don't see what's next until it's placed in our laps. But whatever you're facing right now, know that God has prepared you for this moment.

When people tell you that you're unqualified—no title, no degree, no platform—remember: they weren't there when God brought you through battle after battle. Intelligence is useful. But wisdom from God, born through experience and faith, is powerful.

David's strength came from real life. His wisdom came from God. His authenticity made space for God's glory.

Moses and David both faced family conflicts, personal struggles, and public battles. But through it all, they followed God's plan—and they came out victorious.

God has brought you through some "giant" situations—divorce, loss, sickness, betrayal. Maybe it was a car crash, a difficult surgery, or a season of despair. But through it all, God gave you what you needed.

When God asks, "Whom shall I send?"—you can boldly say, "Here am I, Lord. Send me" (Isaiah 6:8, NIV paraphrased).

Stay focused. There will be distractions—some from people who mean well. But not every strategy is for you. David succeeded because he trusted his calling, not conventional wisdom. He resisted pressure to conform and instead honored God with his authenticity.

We don't need to fight so long or so hard when we fully embrace who God has called us to be and stand on what He has already shown us.

Moses was called because of God's plan for His people. Likewise, David was called not just to slay Goliath but to lead a nation. And you are called—not just to survive your current fight, but to walk in purpose.

Every trial, every lion, every bear has prepared you. Don't let fear make you miss your Goliath moment. There will be more battles after this, so stay focused!

David didn't need Saul's armor (know who you are and remain authentic).

What do you like? What do you enjoy doing? Maybe your family or friends don't enjoy the things you like. Remain authentic. Go and do what you enjoy- find people who like what you like. Don't put on others' garments; don't take on others' ways. Stay true to yourself.

David knew this armor wasn't for him. David knew he just needed what God had already placed in his hands. The stones were already there... waiting for his moment of faith and obedience.

Come what may, you have purpose. Life will bring pain, but it's not about the pain. It's not about the fight. It's about the call.

Spend time in prayer. More fights will come. But every time you fall to your knees, turn your eyes to God. In Him, we grow. In Him, we endure. And through Him, we overcome.

"Can anything ever separate us from Christ's love?... No power in the sky above or in the earth below—indeed, nothing in all creation will ever be able to separate us from the love of God that is revealed in Christ Jesus our Lord" (Romans 8:35-39, NIV).

Hold tight. Stand firm. Stay authentic, Trust God. Because this— every bit of hardship—prepares you for purpose.

Betrayed into the Palace

"You intended to harm me, but God intended it for good to accomplish what is now being done, the saving of many lives." (Genesis 50:20, NIV).

Betrayal. The very word stirs up a deep ache. Whether it's family, friends, or a system we trusted, being betrayed cuts to the core. It's more than just hurt feelings; it's the sting of rejection, the confusion of unexpected loss, and the weight of abandonment. Betrayal makes you question everything: your worth, your purpose, even your identity.

Joseph knew betrayal intimately. Sold into slavery by his own brothers, stripped of his robe, his status, and his home, he was left with nothing but pain. Imagine the heartache of being thrown into a pit by the ones you laughed with, grew up with, and trusted. Their jealousy and rage didn't just take Joseph's freedom; they tried to destroy his future.

And yet… God was with him.

Though he was thrown into the pit, falsely accused, and imprisoned, none of it stopped God's plan. Joseph's story reminds us that betrayal may redirect us, but it can never stop God's purpose. You see, betrayal doesn't cancel your calling—it often catapults it. What Joseph didn't know in the pit was that his journey through pain was the very road that would lead him to the palace. The suffering wasn't a detour; it was preparation.

Let that sink in: What others meant to break you, God can use to build you.

God didn't cause the betrayal, but He allowed it. Why? Because even in betrayal, He is sovereign. He is weaving a story bigger than our wounds—one of redemption, purpose, and hope. The pit may feel like the end, but it's just the beginning.

Joseph eventually stood face-to-face with the very brothers who sold him. But instead of revenge, he offered grace. He had grown. The pit had purified his character. The prison had shaped his faith. And the palace? It was never about power—it was about purpose. Joseph was positioned to save a nation because he trusted God in the pain.

So, if you've been betrayed, take heart. Your pain has not disqualified you—it has positioned you. Your tears are not wasted; your trust is not in vain. What the enemy meant for evil, God is turning for good.

This isn't the end. It's preparation for the promise.

Jesus -Focused and Faithful

Jesus was focused on the fight and faithful to the call.

If the Master of it all had to fight, there is no doubt we will too.

Conflict is inevitable. But we don't have to lose heart or lose focus—because Jesus Christ, the Master, is our perfect example. He shows us how to stand in the fight without letting the fight define us.

Scripture reminds us that our battle is not with people—"flesh and blood"—but "against principalities, against powers, against the rulers of the darkness of this age, against spiritual hosts of wickedness in the heavenly places" (Ephesians 6:12, NIV). The Christian life is a spiritual war. Satan will fight you on every front. He will attack anything and everything to prevent God's will from unfolding in your life. He doesn't want you to even hear hope. He disrupts, deceives, divides, and sows fear so that you can't see or trust what God has planned for you. But Jesus shows us that the fight is not the focus. The call is.

From the start of His ministry, Jesus faced relentless opposition. Temptation in the wilderness. Accusations from religious leaders. Betrayal from close friends. Agony in the Garden. Death on a cross. Yet through it all, He never lost sight of why He came. He remained focused on His mission—redemption and salvation for humanity. He did not fight to be seen. He did not fight to be right. He didn't need to prove anything. He fought for purpose. He fought because of the call.

When Satan tempted Him with shortcuts to glory, Jesus stayed the course. When crowds tried to crown Him king for the wrong reasons, He slipped away. When the Pharisees tried to trap Him with their questions, He answered with wisdom and calm. He faced the attacks but never let them become the assignment.

Jesus shows us how to endure real battles—without being consumed by them. His eyes stayed on the cross, on the Father's will, on the greater purpose. We must learn to do the same.

We need spiritual discernment to know which battles are distractions and which are divine assignments. When we make the fight our focus, we become reactive. But when we keep our eyes on the call, we become anchored in purpose.

Consider King Herod, who ordered the massacre of innocent children in an attempt to stop Jesus before He could even speak. Herod represents the kind of opposition designed not to test you but to eliminate you. And some of us are facing that level of attack, not because we're doing something wrong, but because of the potential locked inside our calling.

The question is not whether opposition will come—it will. The real question is: Will you allow the pressure to pull you away from your purpose, or will you let it push you deeper into it? Jesus chose the latter. So must we.

Jesus faced constant opposition, betrayal, and temptation throughout His life. Yet He never lost sight of His divine assignment—to bring salvation to the world. His example reminds us that while spiritual conflict is guaranteed, it is not the center of our story. The call is.

We are not fighting people. We are up against spiritual forces that seek to stop us from walking in our God-given purpose. But when we look at Jesus, we find both strength and strategy. We learn to fight well, without losing focus. To engage in necessary battles—without being defined by them. To endure opposition—but stay obedient to the call.

Know your assignment. From a young age, Jesus understood He was sent for a higher purpose. At just 12 years old, He told His parents, "Didn't you know I had to be in my father's house?" (Luke 2:49, NIV).

Even before the public knew who He was, Jesus was already aligned with the call, being about His Father's business. He didn't waste time chasing popularity or proving Himself. He was anchored in the Father's purpose, not people's expectations. I know it looks like you don't belong. I know people are wondering why you are here. You are not old enough, you are not educated enough, you don't have all the credentials. But when you are about the Father's business, the Father will seat you in places, even when it looks like it's before your time. But God's time is the perfect time. God's place is the right place.

I Called You

I remember when I started my first administrative job. Looking back, I know without a doubt—it had to be nobody but the Lord who opened that door. I didn't have the experience. I didn't even recognize what God was doing in my life at the time. But doors began to open, and I suddenly found myself in a place where I felt like I didn't belong.

I had just been hired, knowing absolutely nothing about the position. But what I did have was a heart to learn and a willingness to serve. Maybe a week into the job, we had a staff meeting, and I was asked to attend. Can I tell you how afraid and intimidated I felt?

This meeting was full of directors—people with master's degrees and years of experience. Just the thought of sitting in that room overwhelmed me. I was so nervous. I could feel a panic attack creeping in. I didn't know what to expect. I had never been in a staff meeting before. I had never sat at a table with people who didn't look like me or talk like me. I didn't have their credentials or background, and fear began to whisper that I didn't belong.

The morning of the meeting, while getting ready for work, I talked to the Lord about how scared and unworthy I felt. And then, in the middle of my fear, I heard the Holy Spirit speak something so simple—yet so powerful. It dropped all fear from my spirit. He said, "You put your pants on one leg at a time, just like they do. The blood that runs through your veins is as red as the blood that runs through theirs. I have called you to this place." At the time, I didn't fully understand the depth of that word. But it settled me. It grounded me. It reminded me that we're all human, and God had every right to place me in that room—even if I didn't feel qualified.

That simple truth gave me a level playing field. It sounds strange, I know—but the idea that we all get dressed the same way reminded me that I wasn't less than anyone else. And if for no other reason, I was there because I belonged. We all put our pants on the same way.

I giggle about that now, but then, it changed everything. I walked into that meeting, still nervous but with my head held a little higher. I felt like maybe, just maybe, I belonged. And the meeting? It was fine. I was fine. I stayed in that position for over 10 years. God grew me. God matured me. God helped me. God was with me. And now, I know that when God calls you to a place, you don't need to question or fight whether or not you fit in. You put your pants on just like they do. You belong- " I called you to that place."

Jesus stayed in constant communication with the Father. Jesus consistently withdrew to pray, even when crowds were pressing in for miracles.

"But Jesus often withdrew to lonely places and prayed." (Luke 5:16, NIV).

There are times when we allow loneliness to become a distraction. We often view seasons of isolation or silence as something negative when, in fact, those moments can be the perfect opportunity to seek the Father and hear Him more clearly.

For Jesus, prayer wasn't just a side practice or a spiritual routine—it was His lifeline. That's worth repeating. For Jesus, prayer wasn't just a side practice or a spiritual routine—it was His lifeline. It was how He stayed focused. In constant communion with the Father, He received clarity, direction, and strength to keep moving forward. When the fight got loud, He got still—so He could hear heaven.

He Refused Distractions—Even Good Ones.

After feeding thousands and performing miracles, people wanted to make Him king by force (John 6:15, NIV). But Jesus withdrew. Why? Because that wasn't the assignment.

He didn't let fame, applause, or power distract Him from the cross.

Even when Peter tried to talk Him out of going to Jerusalem (where He'd suffer), Jesus rebuked him:
"Get behind me, Satan! You are a stumbling block to me; you do not have in mind the concerns of God, but merely human concerns." (Matthew 16:23, NIV).

Jesus recognized that not every voice—even well-meaning ones—should be followed. If it pulled Him away from the cross, it wasn't from God. Anything that pulls you away from what God has called you to do is not God. We can't put all the blame on others; our own voices and thoughts may not be of God.

If you are more concerned with what others will say or think, it's not God. If you care more about what you will get from it, it may not be God. If you are always excited or see it as something you can most certainly do, it may not be God because some things, most things, that the Lord requires of us are bigger than us. It takes God to move this mountain, it takes God to open this door, it takes God to get you through this. Filter. Every. Fight. Through. Purpose.

Jesus didn't avoid confrontation, but He never fought to be right or prove a point. Whether confronting religious leaders or resisting Satan in the wilderness, Jesus only fought battles that aligned with His call.

When mocked, beaten, and nailed to the cross, He could've called down angels. But He stayed. Why? Because He saw beyond the fight to the fulfillment of the call:
"Father, forgive them..." (Luke 23:34, NIV).
"It is finished." (John 19:30, NIV).
Even in agony, He was focused.

He Endured Because of the Vision

(Hebrews 12:2, NIV) says it all: "For the joy set before Him, He endured the cross..."The joy wasn't the suffering—it was the salvation that would come because of it.

He wasn't focused on the pain. He was focused on the promise. Jesus didn't react—He responded to the Father's will. He didn't chase applause—He pursued obedience. He didn't get distracted by the fight—He stayed faithful to the call.

And because He did, we have life.

Stay Focused On The Call

The fight may be loud, but the call is louder.

At every stage of life—betrayal, rejection, obscurity, temptation, and pressure—the fight will scream for your attention. But the call of God speaks with steady authority.

The enemy wants your focus. Life demands your attention. But God desires your devotion. If there's one lesson that echoes through the lives of Jonah, Moses, David, Joseph, and Jesus, it's this: Don't lose your focus. Focus is the difference between being stuck in a battle and stepping into your purpose. It helps you hear God's whisper when the world is yelling. It keeps you anchored not in chaos but in calling. Without it, we drift. But with it, we advance. Jonah lost focus and ran, but when he refocused, a city was saved.

Moses doubted and stumbled—but when he locked in on God's voice, a nation walked free. David was underestimated—but when he stayed focused on God, Goliath fell.

Joseph was betrayed, but his focus on the dream God gave him lifted him from the pit to the palace. And Jesus—our perfect example—never lost focus. Through temptation, rejection, and crucifixion, His eyes never left the cross. Because He stayed focused, we now have eternal life.

Here's what you must know: The fight is real, but so is your calling. The distractions are loud, but your purpose is louder. The pain is deep, but the promise is deeper. And this is where many lose their way. We begin to believe that life is about the fight—the hardship, the struggle, the opposition. But it's not.

It's not about the fight. It's about the call.

The enemy doesn't fight you over who you are now—he fights you over who you're becoming. The resistance is designed to wear you out, to pull your attention off the cross and onto the conflict. But when you understand the difference, everything shifts. You stop reacting and start discerning. You stop fighting to be right and start fighting to stay aligned. Jesus didn't fight for attention, approval, or control—He stayed focused on His assignment. So must we.

"I press on toward the goal to win the prize for which God has called me heavenward in Christ Jesus." (Philippians 3:14, NIV) So, how do you stay focused when everything around you tries to pull you off course?

Eyes Forward

Paul wrote Philippians 3 from prison. Beaten, betrayed, shipwrecked, and rejected—he had endured nearly every form of suffering. But when he reflects on it all, he doesn't glorify the pain. He doesn't center the fight. He centers the call.

He doesn't describe a battlefield. He describes a race. Not a frantic scramble for survival but a focused pursuit of something higher. The Greek word for press means to pursue with intensity, not to fight against, but to run toward. That's the difference.

Paul teaches us that the call gives meaning to the fight, but the fight is not the focus. He endured not because the struggle disappeared, but because his eyes were locked on the prize: the upward call of God in Christ.

He didn't survive hardship by obsessing over it—he ran through it with a vision that lifted him above it. He had every reason to quit. But Paul never wasted time rehearsing his wounds. He simply said, "I press." Not because the pain had stopped, but because the purpose had become louder.

Set Your Vision

"Set your minds on things above, not on earthly things." (Colossians 3:2, NIV).

This is more than encouragement—it's a command. A mindset shift. Paul reminds us that if we've been raised with Christ, our perspective must rise, too. We don't navigate life driven by what we feel—we live by what we're called to.

The world is noisy. Fights, offenses, and distractions demand our mental attention. But Colossians tells us to "set" our minds—that Greek word means to seek diligently, to direct your thoughts with intention. In other words: Don't react. Realign.

Paul isn't denying that the fight exists. He's telling us not to let it own our thoughts. Your calling is tied to heaven's agenda. It cannot be fulfilled if your focus is always earthbound.

You fight better when you stop obsessing over the battle and start meditating on the mission. The fight will always be loud. But the call must be louder. This is not about ignoring reality—it's about anchoring in what's eternal. When your mind is consumed by what's temporary—fear, drama, offense—you miss what God is calling you to build.

Setting your mind above doesn't mean the fight disappears. It means the fight doesn't define you. You stop living from reaction and start living from revelation. And when your focus is above, the fight can't pull you below.

Distraction Delays Destiny

"Let your eyes look straight ahead; fix your gaze directly before you. Give careful thought to the[a] paths for your feet and be steadfast in all your ways. Do not turn to the right or the left; keep your foot from evil." (Proverbs 4:25-27, NIV).

This is wisdom written like a father to a son. It's a charge to stay the course, to stay focused, because every step matters. The "right" and the "left" in this passage represent detours, distractions, and unnecessary battles. This isn't just about avoiding sin—it's about avoiding side fights that derail your purpose.

You will be tempted to stop and explain yourself. To defend your name. To respond to every offense, every rumor, every accusation. But Proverbs says: Don't look to the side. Keep your gaze forward.

The call is not in the chaos. It's in the course God set before you. Some of us are tired—not because we're disobedient, but because we've been distracted. Fighting battles that were never ours to fight. Carrying burdens that were never ours to bear. Responding to people who were never assigned to our journey.

This Scripture is for the weary. The wounded. The distracted.

Stay locked in.

Don't let betrayal detour you.

Don't let offense reroute you.

Don't let fear make you look away from the road God has already made clear.

This isn't about avoidance. It's about alignment. You weren't called to chase every conflict—you were called to follow the path laid before you.

Eyes on Jesus, Not the Fight

"And let us run with perseverance the race marked out for us, fixing our eyes on Jesus, the pioneer, and perfecter of faith. For the joy set before him he endured the cross...." (Hebrews 12:1-2, NIV).

This passage captures it all: the race, the fight, the focus.

Yes, life includes weight, wounds, and sins that cling to us. But the key to endurance isn't obsessing over what slows us down—it's fixing our eyes on Jesus.

Jesus faced the greatest battle in human history—the cross. But He didn't focus on the pain. He fixed His eyes on joy. On completion. On purpose. He didn't just endure suffering to prove He could survive. He endured because of what was set before Him.
And so must we.

If Jesus had focused on the pain, He would've never made it through the process. But He kept His eyes locked on the outcome: redemption.

You can't run well while staring at the fights, and you won't endure long if your focus is on the fight. Fix your eyes on the one who called you, and the call will carry you.

Run Called, Not Just Tired

Some people are running—but they're running from something. From pain. From people. From past mistakes. But Paul ran toward something: the high call of God. And because he ran with vision, he ran with endurance.

You're not here to fight for survival—you're here to walk in purpose. Yes, the fight will come. But don't live centered on it. Live centered on the call.

Your victory doesn't lie in how well you fight back. It lies in how faithfully you follow forward. So, press not because the battle is over, but because the call is greater.

CHAPTER 7

TRUST THE CALL

You must learn to trust the call even through the pain. You may be going through some callous times right now. Maybe you've been mistreated, lied to, betrayed, or abandoned by people you love dearly. And though it hurts—sometimes so deeply it feels like you'll never recover—you are still on the journey toward God's purpose for your life. Even when your circumstances seem to be the result of other people's wrongdoing, here's the truth: God is working in your heart.

He may be softening you, teaching you forgiveness and grace. Or perhaps He's humbling you, drawing you closer to Him, because let's be honest—many of us don't truly run to God until we're at our wits' end. But hear this clearly: God will take every ounce of your pain—all the lies, rejection, abandonment, and betrayal—and use it to reveal Himself to you in a way you've never known before. He will use it to grow and mature you for the call.

A Picture of God's Process

Joseph couldn't afford to be childish, arrogant, impatient, or unforgiving in the palace. His new God-given position demanded maturity. He could have stood before his brothers and said, "Now I have you where I want you. You need me, but I remember when you left me." He had every right, every ounce of power and authority, to get revenge. But that wouldn't have represented the heart of God.

The journey to Joseph's purpose was long and painful, but it was intentional. God was preparing him for something greater. And in the same way, God is preparing you.

He's building in you the character that reflects His heart: humility, grace, mercy, patience, love, and the strength that comes through forgiveness. It doesn't mean the journey is easy. It doesn't erase the pain. But it does mean that God has not forgotten you.

You're not behind. You're not disqualified.

You're just being formed. It's not about the fight. It's about the call.

The Moment It Shifted for Me

I remember going to church one night during choir rehearsal. They were going around asking everyone to share a Scripture— any Scripture. When it got to me, I froze. I didn't know what to say. But even in that moment, I knew deep down there had to be more to life than what I was experiencing. I didn't know what "more" looked like. I just knew I wanted it. I longed to discover it, to be a part of it.

When God first called me to ministry, I had no idea what that meant. No one in my family was in ministry. I didn't have a model to look up to. So, for years, I hid it in my heart. Around the age of 12, I had a vision. I was riding in the backseat of a car, and we passed a park. Next to it was a wide, beautiful field with vibrant green grass. Suddenly, I saw myself standing on a massive black stage in the middle of that field. Bright lights beamed down like stadium lights. People filled the entire field, sitting, standing, stretching all the way to the sidewalks. I held a microphone and preached. Others stood on the stage with me, but I don't know if they were preachers or just part of what God was doing. That vision has stayed with me ever since. Every time I pass that park, I remember it.

I don't know if I'll ever preach in that exact field. But I believe I might. Either way, I know the call is bigger than me. I've stood on many stages since then, delivering messages of hope, love, forgiveness, and salvation. But it all started with that seed planted in a young heart with no clear direction but a strong sense of destiny.

Called to Endure

Remember I shared earlier that I was at a women's conference.

How afraid and inadequate I felt. I didn't know if God could use me. I tried to study. I tried to be prepared, but I couldn't seem to get comfortable. Preachers, teachers, and presenters know exactly what I mean. I was a total wreck. Sitting there, I couldn't hear God for my own thoughts and worries. I felt sick and unprepared, although I had been up all night studying and trying to hear a word from the Lord. Now, I'm at the conference, on the front row, scared out of my mind. Should I walk out? Should I say I'm sick? I'm having all these thoughts, but I couldn't move. It was like the Holy Spirit had super-glued me to the seat. I looked around the room at all the beautiful women—some I deeply admired—who looked for me for a word I didn't have, and I felt so unworthy.

I was now being introduced, and I just stayed in a fog. I wasn't present; I wasn't there at all. I said, "Lord help me!" I whispered a prayer, "Lord, I'm so scared. Lord, please help me. Speak to me, speak through me, speak for me."

I cannot tell you what all I said. I vaguely remember what I preached about, but I remember coming to a close, and I kept saying. " It's not about the fight but the call."

If God could use Moses—with all his insecurities and limitations—He can use you.

As the women approached me, so many thanked me for coming and told me how they enjoyed the word, and they kept repeating. "It's not about the fight; it's about the call. That certainly wasn't my title, but the Lord spoke, and He wanted me and those in the room to know that.

I gave God glory then, and I give God the glory today for bringing me through that. I thank God for using me and not allowing me to be embarrassed or an embarrassment to Him, to those who invited me, for not allowing me to embarrass my pastor at that time, my husband, and my family. Thank you, Lord, for being with me, speaking to me, and speaking through me.

That night, I fell into bed absolutely exhausted. My sweet Victor made sure I had all that I needed and told me I'd given a great message and that he was proud of me. He said, "God really used you today." I wept. I was encouraged, thankful, relieved, and tired. I was glad that was over.

The next morning, I shared with Victor that I believed the Lord wanted me to write a book called It's Not About the Fight But the Call. I wasn't sure, but I felt strongly about it. As time went on, I wrestled with the thought. As we talked about it, Victor was excited, and he always believed in me and encouraged me.

That was over 14 years ago, I believe. I tried and tried. I would write, then stop. I'd start again, then quit. I would run, stay up half the night, and still give up. I was excited—then I felt unworthy. I'd sit down to write, only to feel blocked and unable to continue. I tried not to write this book. I put it away and counted it as something, maybe I just wanted to do. But then the Lord would impress upon me to write. So many nights, He would wake me and remind me: Write

I cried and cried because this was bigger than me. It was more than I thought I was capable of—and it was. I couldn't do it. The Lord had to speak to me, through me, and for me. Reminder after reminder. Conviction and restlessness. They kept showing up. I'd have faith, then lose faith. But I kept on "faithing." I kept on writing. I would put it down, write a page, then trash it. I'd write a paragraph, then delete it. I'd pray and cry. I'd ask the Lord what to write. Sometimes, I would only get out a sentence or a paragraph at a time.

I stopped worrying about it. I stopped trying to get it all right. I stopped stressing over whether I'd ever finish it. But I didn't stop. I kept asking God to help me. "God, if this is You—help me. Show me how." I asked Him not to let this be me, but to let it be what

He wanted from me. This book was a fight. But I knew—it was about a greater call.

While you're not called to chase fights, you are called to endure them. Struggles are real, but they should not distract us from our heavenly assignment. God won't give up on you. Didn't give up on me. What He calls you to, He will help you, be with you, and see you through.

We must fight not against people but against the spiritual forces seeking to derail our purpose. We fight against ourselves and the lies we believe because maybe we haven't seen it modeled through our families or those around us. We must leave those and get around those who are doing what we desire to do. Get around people who have fought through and made it. Learn from them. How did they remain focused? How did they make it?

Through my own personal trials, divine appointments, and God's sustaining power, I am here. You are called to remain focused—trusting God's plan, not fighting your way through, but "faithing" your way through.

CHAPTER 8

GOD PREPARES
BEFORE HE POSITIONS

I've lived enough life to say this with confidence: God doesn't give you the weight of your calling without first strengthening your shoulders to carry it. When I look back at all I've seen, heard, and endured—the highs, the heartbreaks, the holy moments—I now realize that much of it was preparation. God was shaping me for something I couldn't fully see yet. I was living through training grounds long before I had the vocabulary to call it ministry.

I've preached in places without pulpits, led people without recognition, and served in silence without applause. And you know what? That was the call, too. Because the call comes before the title. Always.

I believe God is kind enough not to throw us into something great without first forming us to survive it. He is intentional. He is wise. And He prepares us behind the scenes before He places us on any platform.

So, hear this: Trust Him with the call. Believe that He's the one who called you. Obey what He tells you to do. The calling, the responsibility, the anointing—it's all from Him. And He doesn't just give you what you need to start. He equips you to walk in it boldly, own it fully, and finish it faithfully.

The Call Always Comes First

The call is anything and whatever the Lord has impressed on your heart, whatever you have passion and convictions about. Maybe you feel called to encourage and help others. Maybe you enjoy baking or cleaning. Maybe you have a gift for singing, painting, or dancing. How does the Lord impress on your heart to use your gifts? I would even go as far as to ask, "What have you been through?" God can use your pain, disappointments, and lack to help and encourage others. Let me take you back to a few people God called long before anyone ever gave them a title:

David – Called and Anointed Before the Crown

"Samuel took the horn of oil and anointed him in the presence of his brothers, and from that day on, the Spirit of the Lord came powerfully upon David" (1 Samuel 16:13, NIV).

David was just a shepherd boy when God chose him.

He wasn't a king yet. He didn't live in a palace. But that didn't matter—because God doesn't wait for titles to affirm a call. David was anointed in the presence of people who didn't believe in him, yet that anointing stayed with him through battles, betrayal, and years of running from Saul. David's title came later. His call came first.

Jeremiah – Appointed Before Birth

"Before I formed you in the womb I knew[a] you, before you were born I set you apart; I appointed you as a prophet to the nations." (Jeremiah 1:5, NIV).

Before Jeremiah ever spoke a word to Israel, God had already spoken a word over him. He didn't need a pulpit or a platform to be called. God gave him purpose before he ever took a breath. And that purpose wasn't something Jeremiah could earn—it was something he was born into.

Paul – Called by Grace, Not by Position

"But when God, who set me apart from my mother's womb and called me by his grace, was pleased to reveal his Son in me so that I might preach him among the Gentiles, my immediate response was not to consult any human being." (Galatians 1:15-16, NIV).

Paul's story is powerful. He wasn't just not in ministry—he was actively persecuting it. But one divine encounter shifted everything. He didn't go to seminary first. He didn't seek approval from the apostles. He stepped into his calling because God said go. His transformation didn't come with a title—it came with grace.

Jesus – The Called One, Not Just the Named One

"The Spirit of the Lord is upon Me, because He has anointed Me to preach the gospel…" (Luke 4:18, NIV).

Even Jesus declared His call before He was recognized by many. He read the scroll, proclaimed the truth, and stepped fully into His mission—

even as people doubted, rejected, and ridiculed Him. His assignment didn't come from their acceptance. It came from the father.

Purpose Before Position

Your calling doesn't begin with public confirmation. It begins with divine conviction. The anointing is real—even when no one sees it. The responsibility is sacred—even when no one applauds it. And the authority is legitimate, even when it hasn't been acknowledged by people. The call is divine. The title is public. One gives you purpose. The other gives you position. But position means nothing without purpose.

Time Is Sacred

I often think of (Matthew 24:36, NIV), where Jesus says: "But about that day or hour no one knows, not even the angels in heaven, nor the Son, but only the Father." We don't know how long we have to walk this calling out. When I think of this scripture, I don't just think of it as death only. I mean, we don't know the day or the hour of death. But your "last day" might be the day before your strength changes. The day before your eyesight fades. The day before your voice is gone. We assume we'll always have the time to do something. But anything can happen, anything can change, and you may not be able to complete the call. You may complete the journey, but will you complete the call?

We don't know, but Jesus reminds us that "As long as it is day, we must do the works of him who sent me. Night is coming, when no one can work" (John 9:4, NIV).

In other words, don't wait. Don't get distracted. Don't wait for a title. Don't wait for confirmation. Don't wait until people believe in you. Don't get sidetracked. Whatever God called you to, RUN. If He anointed you, MOVE. If He whispered your name, ANSWER. You don't need permission to walk in what God has already prepared. He's been getting you ready behind the scenes. So, when the door opens, don't question it. Don't shrink. Don't second-guess your worth. You've been called. And the preparation was proof.

CHAPTER 9

NO MASK, NO APOLOGIES

I am called to be me. No more masks and no more apologies. When you reach this place in life, you've reached freedom. You've tried to fit in; you've gone along to get along. You accepted mistreatment, side remarks, and uncomfortable comments. You've been mishandled and mistreated. You've worn the mask of smiling and covering up to keep others happy and comfortable. No more masks and no more apologies.

When you walk in the truth of who God created you to be, you become harder to distract? You stop chasing false versions of success. You stop comparing your journey to someone else's. Instead of being sidetracked by the noise around you, you remain focused on your calling. Authenticity causes distraction to lose its grip because you know what matters. Your heart is anchored in purpose, not in performance or people-pleasing.

Let's be honest—how many times have you changed who you were to fit into someone else's expectations? Maybe it was something as small as giving up your favorite hobby because the people around you didn't enjoy it. Maybe you love swimming, but your circle doesn't, so you stopped. You didn't want to be the outlier, so you gave in. But here's the thing: every time we shrink ourselves for others, we move further away from the person God called us to be.

Authenticity says, "I don't need to be everywhere, do everything, or please everyone—I just need to be where God has placed me, doing what He's called me to do." When you live authentically, you're aligned with God's truth, not the lies the enemy whispers. Deception thrives in confusion and insecurity. But when you're rooted in who God says you are, you begin to recognize the enemy's lies before they even take root.

I've had moments where people questioned my decisions, not realizing that what didn't make sense to them was actually obedience to God for me. When I left a full-time job for a part-time position, people thought I was crazy. And to them, maybe it looked like a step back. But the truth is, God was calling me to a deeper level of purpose—one that required space, surrender, and faith. My authenticity didn't need to be explained. It just needed to be lived. The call of God on your life will rarely make sense to the crowd. But it doesn't have to. They've got their own calling to understand. You don't need their permission—just God's direction.

Authenticity is Warfare

In these times—and honestly, as it's always been—it can be a struggle to truly know who you are. We compare ourselves to others. We see what they're doing and feel like we need to be doing something, too. The truth is, it takes time to figure out who you are, what you want, and where you're going.

But once you begin to discover that—and you start walking in it—being your authentic self becomes an act of spiritual resistance. Why? Because every time you choose truth over appearance, purpose over pressure, and identity over insecurity, you're waging war against the enemy's two favorite weapons: distraction and deception.

We live in a world full of distractions—some of them even look good on the surface. You're encouraged to hustle harder, be at every event, lead multiple ministries, chase dual majors, and say yes to every opportunity. But if you're not careful, you'll end up performing more than you're obeying. You'll do what looks impressive but feels empty.

But authenticity keeps you grounded in purpose. It helps you discern when something is just busyness dressed up as opportunity. Taking a class or joining a club just because your circle is doing it might win you approval, but it may not align with God's assignment for you.

When you're true to your authentic self, you're living from the inside out, not the outside in. You're not chasing what looks good to others; you're following what God planted in you.

Authenticity says: "I choose who God made me to be, not who the world says I should be." Deception, on the other hand, wants you to doubt your worth. It wants you to question your calling. It whispers, "You're not enough," or, "Who do you think you are?" But authenticity stands firm in who God says you are—even when life tries to convince you otherwise.

Spiritual resistance doesn't always look like casting out demons or standing behind a pulpit. Sometimes, it looks like quietly choosing obedience when no one understands your decision. Sometimes, it means walking a road others don't recognize, knowing full well that their yellow brick road won't lead you home. Only God's path for you will."

And let me tell you, that path requires focus. You can't run your race with power if you're constantly switching lanes, trying to impress the crowd. Stay in your lane. Run your race. Walk in your truth. Because when you live authentically:

Your motives become pure.

Your obedience becomes sustainable.

Your purpose becomes life-giving.

You can't keep up a mask forever. But you can sustain purpose when you're living from your true identity in Christ. God doesn't anoint the version of you that performs—He anoints the real you. The one He called. The one He formed. The one He sees, even when others don't understand.

Comparison fades when you're grounded in who you are. Authenticity silences the pressure to compete by anchoring your value in your calling, not in competition. "Authenticity anchors you. Imitation distracts you. Truth propels you and keeps you FOCUSED."

Strange – but God Is Still Working

"Beloved, think it not strange concerning the fiery trial which is to try you, as though some strange thing happened unto you: "But rejoice inasmuch as you participate in the sufferings of Christ, so that you may be overjoyed when his glory is revealed." (1 Peter 4:12-13, NIV).

The fight can often feel strange—unfair, confusing, disorienting—but God's call is not shaken by what seems strange to us. If we only trusted God when life made sense, we wouldn't need faith. But in all the strange things that happen in our lives, the faith journey becomes real.

When you read the Word of God, there is one hardship, an unfortunate, painful story after another. The scriptures give a look inside of real life. We are not exempt from trouble. The scriptures also command us not to be surprised by the fires we face. If we can get to a place where we expect the walk to be easy because we're faithful, because we are good people, then we set ourselves up for spiritual disappointment. This passage says: Don't be thrown off by trials. Expect them. I'm not sure where we've learned we won't go through. I know we say we are going to trust in God, yet we are restless, sleepless, angry, and revengeful because of the fiery trials. You are not being abandoned in the fiery trials—you are being refined.

We know how suffering felt for our savior. He endured and came through, and He will see you through. It's okay to be surprised, overwhelmed, or confused. I know it's not always popular to say things like this. But the truth is, it doesn't matter your age or status; life takes us all by surprise. We are overwhelmed, and sometimes we just can't make sense of it. Even strong believers feel this way. But you must not allow strange to turn into stuck.

You will have trouble and still have joy.

That's not denial. This is a promise. Jesus didn't say "maybe" you'll face trouble. He said, "You will have trouble." But He also said you can overcome because He already has. In hard moments, we must ask ourselves and God, "What are you forming in me?" not "When will this stop?" I have tried to rush through my hard season; I have tried to make it all go away. Over time, with each issue of life, I've grown to not always say, "Lord, get me out of this or take this away," but "How can I stay faithful in it? How can I not waver in my faith? How can I keep my focus on you and not the circumstances?" My prayer becomes, "Lord, show me what you are doing. Lord, keep me faithful to you. Lord, help me to stand, help me to have joy, help me not to pay more attention to what hurts and what's scary more than I put on you."

I wish I could tell you there is a formula for walking this journey. The only formula is your faith in God. All the praying I did for my husband. I thought losing my husband was the final blow. I felt like my pain had hit the ceiling; life handed me more uncertainty, more battles, more "strange" moments, but my prayers and belief in God weren't in vain. Even though my husband was not healed the way I hoped, my faith did not fail me. It had nothing to do with me, but everything to do with God being present and with me all the way.

I was able to keep walking. I kept trusting because my focus shifted from the pain to the purpose. Victor was my lord-my leader, my protector, my provider, my best friend, my only help in this life. He believed in me and supported me. But I recognized who my Lord was. The keeper of my soul, the one who loved me more, who could protect me better, who would provide for me all along, and who held the key to my past, present, and future. I trust Him, and I focus on Him.

Life is like a garden and a gardener. Can you imagine a gardener digging up soil in her garden? To the untrained eye or unfamiliar gardener, it all looks destructive. It appears that the ground is being ruined. But the gardener knows the soil has to be broken. It has to be disrupted before the seeds can rest in softer ground and take root. That's exactly how life feels sometimes. It feels strange. Disruptive. Like God is tearing up everything you depended on. But what if He's just preparing the ground for seeds in your next season? So don't think it strange. Think of it as part of your process. What feels strange to you may just be strategic to God."

Stand, Worship, and Believe

Your issues, frustrations, pain, or lack isn't the focus—faith is.

You don't have to worry about all the issues because your faith is in God.

"I have told you these things, so that in me you may have peace. In this world you will have trouble. But take heart! I have overcome the world." (John 16:33, NIV).

I desire to remind you that the battle is real, but it's not where our attention should rest. We aren't so super spiritual that we're blind to what's happening, or our thoughts don't go toward all the things that concern us, worry us, or upset us, but our Faith isn't about fighting harder—it's about trusting God deeper. I have been there- exhausted, discouraged, and afraid of what's ahead. Life can feel overwhelming—growing old alone, facing the world alone, handling bills and home repairs alone. But just as I've had to reassure myself, I want to reassure you: you're not alone. My strength, my future, my life isn't in my hands- Your strength, future, life isn't in your hands—it's in your faith, in God.

In 2 Chronicles 20 (NIV), Jehoshaphat was surrounded by enemies (FIGHTS). He did not provoke them, and he could not defeat them on his own. The odds were against him. But instead of focusing on the fight, he focused on the CALL to seek the Lord, and God delivered the victory in a way no military strategy ever could. This shows us that it doesn't matter how smart or experienced you are, there are some hard places only the Lord can bring you through."

Sometimes, our issues and pain overtake us. There seems to be more bills than money, more stress than rest. Jehoshaphat and the people of Judah had multiple armies coming against them. There was no natural way out... I've acted in my own knowledge and in what seemed to be the most logical and thought, I can move this to pay that bill. I can turn that off to be able to support that need. I can help them by taking on their responsibilities.

What a mess I made. Like the people of Judah, I was afraid. Jehoshaphat didn't start sharpening swords—he didn't move bills around or trade one problem for another. He called for a fast and prayer. Jehoshaphat shows us that the fight wasn't physical—it was spiritual. Faith and focus are our strategy, not force.

It's not about how hard the battle is, but how clearly we obey God's call.

The call for Judah wasn't to fight—it was to stand, worship, and believe. I know some things are just worth repeating. The call for Judah wasn't to fight— it wasn't for them to figure out their own way, take charge, or react, but it was to stand, worship, and believe.

How many times have you read, "Do not be afraid or discouraged... for the battle is not yours, but God's?" We read this, we say these things, but we stand, worship, and believe.

In verse 17 of 2 Chronicles, they were told to take their positions and stand firm, not swing swords, not to fight. "Faith isn't proven by avoiding battles—it's proven by how you trust God in them." Trust in the Lord in whatever you are facing today. You may be surrounded by fear, grief, doubt, or loss. Friends, health, family, and money may have left you high and dry. You may have no strategy that makes human sense, but like Jehoshaphat, you're still called to show up, take your position in worship and faith, and let God do what only He can do.

Sometimes, we've done all we can do. I prayed. I fasted. I took communion. I called in the prayer warriors. I believed for healing for my husband. Like Jehoshaphat, I stood in faith. I'd seen God do miracles; I trusted He would do a miracle for us. But the outcome was not what I asked for; it was not what I wanted at all. But I can say, God still showed Himself strong in the fight. I saw how God worked some things out just for me along the way, I see how God is still with me today, and I'm believing Him for greater! So, I remain, standing, worshiping, and believing.

Make no mistake about it. The enemy didn't win. Death didn't win. Because, in the moment, God called my sweet husband home. The Lord gave me the grace and the strength to keep standing. Like Jehoshaphat did for the people of Judah, I desire to lead others in how to trust God's plan even when the fight feels overwhelming, lonely, and hard.

Even when the answer isn't what I hoped for, God's purpose is still working. His plan is still perfect. His call on our lives is still in motion. And I can still stand in worship and walk in victory." It's not over for me on this journey, and it's not over for you. God may not remove our battles, but He will remove the burden to fight them in our own strength, so as I'm moving ahead, let us stop striving and start trusting. Whatever you're facing, be it uncertainty, rejection, or fear, don't let the fight scare you, and don't let the call intimidate you. Your faith in God makes you secure in both.

CONCLUSION

I was given the title of this book over twelve years ago, and I tried to ignore the call to write it, but it kept coming back. Everything that could have hindered me from writing this book happened.

I can confess now that most of it was my fault. As soon as I would sit to start writing, the phone would ring, the TV would catch my attention, or I would feel like I needed to check my email or see what was happening on social media. I would remember I needed to run to the store. I would get hungry and decide to cook. I would get tired and decide to go to bed. So many things would show up each time I tried to write, and I would get distracted by them. I tried to write the book, but I just could not get my words to sound right. I tried ignoring this call because I felt like I wasn't a writer; I believed the lie of the devil who told me I had nothing to say.

Isn't it strange that you always have time to do nothing? That there's always time in your life for random frivolous things. There's always time in your life to waste time, but when it's time to go to work, when it's time to serve the Lord, when it's time to practice the piano or write a book (my personal fight), it's like you just don't have the wherewithal or the energy to do it. Everything comes up, everything distracts you. Even though it may sound strange, it's really not because it's the enemy at work. It is the enemy of your destiny, and it is the lie that we believe that we can't do it.

There is always some fear, anxiety, or feeling of unworthiness that keeps us from doing what God has assigned for our lives. But do you not realize that if God did not want you to do this–whatever this may be–that he would not have put the call in you? Because he put the call in you, he has given you everything you need to accomplish it.

However, because we live in this world that has all these

distractions and all these things we could be doing instead– things that will fulfill us for the moment but will do nothing for our purpose– we have no time for what God has called us to do. So we have a choice: we can spend our life sitting, watching TV, playing video games, watching other people succeed in their lives on social media, being distracted from God's call, or we can get up and be about our Father's business.

When you're avoiding going about your Father's business, you know it in your spirit. You know in your heart of hearts that the separation from God that you have allowed will affect you spiritually and physically. You may not rest well at night. You may feel anxious and unsettled.

When you are resting at night. But God wants you to understand that you have something to say in your song, in your writing, in your dancing, in your creativity, in your art, in your poetry, in your glass-making, in your teaching. You have something that at least one person needs, and if it helps them, if it delivers them, saves them, or sets them free, you have done what God has called you to do. But in order to do it, in order to believe in yourself, believe in God, and not be distracted, you must stay focused.

It wasn't until I focused and stopped worrying that I believed in God. I was obedient, one sentence at a time. I reached out for help, and people took advantage of me. I trusted others with what God told me to do. I didn't know what I was doing. But even through being lied on, taken advantage of, and talked about, I got it. I began to trust God and turn all my attention and focus on him. I'm not angry or upset with anyone. I'm grateful to all who tried. It was the fight that brought me here. I had to set my mind on God. "Set your minds on things above, not on earthly things" (Colossians 3:2, NIV).

Paul teaches us in Colossians that we should set our minds on spiritual things. We often set our minds on what others say about us, what others think about us, and what's going on around us– earthly things– but we must learn to set our minds on Christ. Christ is the only solid thing we have, and he should be the very center of our focus. When we have unpleasant issues and hard circumstances, we begin to concentrate on how we can fix them in our own strength, but we really should be concentrating on Jesus Christ and what pleases him.

I tried to write this book. I started and stopped, and I tried to come at it another way. I started over again and again. I started over so many times because I just wasn't sure how to write a book. I knew it was something that God had called me to, but I felt like I just couldn't articulate what I was hearing the Lord say. I didn't know how it would come across in a book, but each time I wrote a page, I would put it away because of the fight of self-doubt. However, because of the call to write this book, I encouraged myself, repeating what I knew: "This is not about me."

It's not about the fight. The call of God on your life is greater than what you are facing. It's not about what they said; It's about the call. It is greater than what you are feeling at this moment. I can tell you, even now, I'm living out this book.

The title of this book has become my life's anthem and my own psalm.

Everyone close to me uses this book title as their anthem to keep going and to regain their focus. God has called you, and He has given you everything you need to carry out your purpose. God has given you everything you need to come through and to get through every difficult place. God has a purpose for all, and you can now believe in God and accomplish His will for your life. Writing in this book has been challenging. I have come to learn that nothing that we do for God is easy or comes easy; in fact, it comes with a price. It comes with fights. There are people in your life who may not even know you, but do not like you. And it's not that they don't like you. The enemy understands the power and the call that you have on your life to accomplish God's will to make a difference and a change in the lives of others, and in this evil and sinful world. Thus, the desire is to stop you and to distract you. Writing this book has been a constant reminder that, through my tears and disappointments, this walk of life is bigger than me. Through my sad days and hard days, this book writing has reminded me and sustained me to keep going because the hand of God, the guidance of God, and the perfect will of God supersedes me.

I have felt alone, disappointed, rejected, and forgotten about more times than I can count. Unappreciated, undervalued, unseen, unheard. But this book has been a constant in my life to get up and put one foot in front of the other to keep my focus on the Lord: His promises, His Word, his love, and the future He has for me.

We often want everything to be about us: what we want, when we want it, how we want it, where we want it. There's been this saying that I've heard all my life from people who reach a certain age of 18 or 21: I'm grown, as though "I'm grown "gives you permission to do what you want to do. This life is not about us. This life is not about what we want or how we feel. It really does not matter your age. We must come to the Father like little children, or we will never enter the Kingdom of Heaven (Matthew 18, NIV).

We must forget and turn aside the things of this world. Even the world views and desires, and we must become like little children– innocent, unashamed, with humility and sincerity in our hearts; we must become helpless and unknowing. Too often, we come to the Father like we know everything. We have already concluded that we have all the answers, but we must come to the Father unknowingly, only knowing what we cannot do without him, and that he is the supplier of every need. Every want is only because He allows it. And this book has been a constant reminder to me that I'm nothing without the Father. I can do nothing without the

Father. I cannot win life's battles without the Father.

As I'm writing these words, my life surrounded by uncertainty, struggles, and pain, I'm reminded in this very moment that "it's not about the fight." If the words on these pages help just one person… If one person sings the anthem, "It's not about the fight, but the call,"… If one person reminds themselves, in times of difficulty, that it's not about the fight, but about the call… If one person chooses to turn their focus back to the Lord, then my labor has not been in vain. I pray that even one person realizes there is something far greater in store for them. God will use this. And He will get the glory.

Don't give up. Don't stop. I know it's been rough. It feels unbearable—unreal at times. You've asked, "Why? "How come? "Why me?" There may never be an answer, or not the one you were hoping for. But I do know this: It's bigger than you. The enemy of dysfunction, perverseness, anger, abuse, and confusion will not and cannot win. He has not won. Victory is in the Lord Jesus.

If you yield it to God and trust the Lord with whatever you are facing or have faced, it can work for good. It can help someone else. It can forgive; it can let go of its hold on you. It can set you free. It can heal. And most of all, it can glorify God.

Trust God with it. The fight was to distort your vision. To delay your obedience. To discourage your faith. To drain your strength. To diminish your worth. To derail your purpose. To divide your focus. To deafen you to God's voice. To discredit your calling. To deceive you into thinking the fight was the end of the story. But it wasn't. It is not because God's call is greater.

ABOUT THE AUTHOR

Minister Betty Booker is a devoted servant of the Kingdom of God—authentic, bold, Spirit-led, and unwavering in her conviction that the Word of God must meet people where they are. Known for her dynamic voice, passionate teaching, and spiritual insight, Betty delivers messages that cut through life's noise and point people back to purpose. As a teacher, preacher, and speaker, her life's mission is to help others remain focused on the call—the call to surrender to Jesus, to live for Him, to serve others, and to walk out purpose even when the fight gets hard.

Born and raised in Athens, Georgia, Betty is a proud 1986 graduate of Clarke Central High School. In 1991, she married Victor Booker, and together they raised two daughters.

Betty surrendered fully to the call of ministry. She faithfully completed her ministerial training through her local church, preached her initial sermon and was licensed in December 2012 January 2019 she was set apart, affirmed by the Church and ordained. Her journey in ministry has been marked by steadfast obedience, spiritual growth, and an unshakable commitment to the assignments God has placed on her life.

She currently serves as the Ministry Trainer at Great Life Ministries, where she equips leaders to walk in excellence, clarity, and spiritual maturity. For seven years, she also served as the Evangelism and Outreach Ministry Assistant. Betty is also the Director of Operations at a local nonprofit, where she ministers to the underserved with the Word of God and hope. Her work extends beyond the pulpit, offering compassion in action and faith that meets practical needs.

Betty's passion is simple yet profound: to encourage everyone to become their best, God-authored selves. She loves sharing the Word of God, offering encouragement, and helping others rediscover hope and focus. She has a unique, Spirit-led ability to speak life, awaken purpose, and declare truth into the hearts of those she encounters—empowering them to walk boldly in all that God has for their lives.

Through this book and workbook, Betty's heartfelt prayer is that the people of God will get their focus back. She believes with all her heart that God has great plans for each of us—and that it's time for men and women to take their attention off life's hardships and refocus on the One who reigns over every hard area. Pain, disappointment, and unfair treatment will always exist. People will oppose you. Grief and heartache are not a matter of if but when. Yet none of these can derail a life that is anchored in calling and committed to Christ.

Betty has served in many ministry capacities, including women's ministry leader, Sunday School, and Bible study teacher, and corporate prayer leader. Her influence spans generations as she continues to mentor and disciple women with wisdom, warmth, and Holy Spirit power.

Her beloved husband and ministry partner, Victor, passed away just weeks before their 30th wedding anniversary after a courageous battle with glioblastoma. Though she has endured deep loss, Betty has never lost sight of her divine assignment. Her resilience, faith, and unwavering devotion continue to inspire all who know her.

Betty continues to serve with humility, purpose, and passion.

Cherished Scripture:

"He that comes to God must believe that He is, and that He is a rewarder of those who diligently seek Him."(Hebrews 11:6, NIV)

Life Verses:

"Everyone will hate you because of me, but the one who stands firm to the end will be saved." (Mark 13:13, NIV)

"I don't look back; I lengthen my stride and reach forward to what is before me."(Philippians 3:13, NIV paraphrased)

SYNOPSIS

FOCUS: It's Not About the Fight, But the Call is a powerful, Spirit-led guide for anyone navigating hardship, transition, or spiritual warfare. In this bold and honest book, Minister Betty Booker invites you to shift your attention from life's battles to God's greater purpose.

Through biblical truth, personal testimony, and heartfelt encouragement, Betty reminds us that while the struggles are real, they are not the point—the call is.

Each chapter challenges you to examine what you're really fighting, recognize distractions and deception, and remember that God often prepares us in private before positioning us in purpose.

Betty writes not from perfection but from lived experience. Her transparency invites you to stop performing, start obeying, and stay anchored in faith—even when it's hard.

If you've ever felt stuck in the fight, this book is your invitation to realign with purpose and walk boldly in your God-given assignment.